The Net-Works Guide to
Creating a Website

A beginner's guide to publishing professional looking pages on the World Wide Web

Tim Ireland

NET-WORKS

PO BOX 200
Harrogate
HG1 2YR
England

www.net-works.co.uk
Email: sales@net-works.co.uk
Fax: +44 (0) 1423 526035

Net.Works is an imprint of Take That Ltd

ISSN: 1-873668-84-8

Text Copyright ©2000 Tim Ireland
Design & Layout Copyright ©2000 Take That Ltd

All rights reserved around the world. This publication is copyright and may not be reproduced, in whole or in part, in any manner (except for excerpts thereof for bona fide purposes in accordance with the Copyright Act) without the prior consent in writing from the Publisher.

10 9 8 7 6 5 4 3 2 1

Trademarks:
Trademarked names are used throughout this book. Rather than place a trademark symbol in every occurance of a trademark name, the names are being used only in an editorial fashion for the benefit of the trademark owner, with no intention to infringe the trademark.

Printed and bound in The United Kingdom.

Disclaimer:
The information in this publication is distributed on an "as is" basis, without warranty. While very effort has been made to ensure that this book is free from errors or omissions, neither the author, the publisher, or their respective employees and agents, shall have any liability to any person or entity with respect to any liability, loss or damage caused or alleged to have been caused directly or indirectly by advice or instructions contained in this book or by the computer hardware or software products described herein. **Readers are urged to seek prior expert advice before making decisions, or refraining from making decisions, based on information or advice contained in this book.**

TTL books are available at special quantity discounts to use as premiums and sales promotions. For more information, please contact the Director of Special Sales at the above address or contact your local bookshop.

Contents

Introduction 4

Chapter 1 - Why Build A Web Site? 6
For business or pleasure?

Chapter 2 - What You Need 8
Computer, Connection, Web Space, Software, Skills Etc.

Chapter 3 - Research 11
Looking at sites across the board, good and bad, with a focus on those of your competitors/contemporaries

Chapter 4 - Content 15
What to put on your site

Chapter 5 - Drafting Your Pages 22
How to construct a plan of your site and make the most of your information

Chapter 6 - Writing For The Web 27
Writing the words for your page - 'Less Is More, More Or Less'.

Chapter 7 - Graphics 32
Different options for making/getting graphics for your page - focus on making your own, repeating graphics, file size etc.

Chapter 8 - Making Your Template 39
How to begin putting together your pages

Chapter 9 - Making Your Site 53
Putting it all together - 'step-by-step'

Continued

Chapter 10 - Checking Your Site 57
Checking your site offline - shortcomings and html mistakes

Chapter 11 - Final Touches 62
Page title, meta tags and such html extras - step-by-step how to draft and insert these tlements.

Chapter 12 - Going Live 68
Using WS_FTP To Upload Your Site And Doing A Quick 'Online' Test

Chapter 13 - Submitting To Search Engines 75
Some tips and tricks for faster, cheaper submission - and better placement

Chapter 14 - The Future 80
A few ideas for the future: counters, polls, shopping facilities etc that you can add simply by cutting and pasting html into your page(s).

Chapter 15 - Some Helpful Web Sites 83
Sites that make putting together and improving your site easier and less complicated

Glossary 97

The book is aimed at everyone who may want to create a website: individuals, businesses and non-commercial organisations. However, the main emphasis will be on building a site for a fictional commercial organisation.

Introduction

Chances are that you think you know nothing of the principles of Inclined Projectile Motion. But you'd be wrong.

When a ball is thrown in the air there are a number of competing forces acting upon it. By knowing the size and direction of these forces you can use a mathematical formula to gauge the distance, height and speed of the ball at any given moment. Then, by solving a quadratic equation, you can judge when and where the ball will land.

Sounds complex, doesn't it? But YOU can, and do, perform these difficult calculations in a fraction of a second without ever going near a calculator. Indeed, you do it every time you catch a ball or hit it with a racket, simply by using your eyes and natural judgement.

Similarly, you do not need to know all about HTML to be able to build a web site. Thanks to the many user-friendly authoring programs that are available, making web pages is often as simple as typing. Still, there are a few tricks to learn if you want your site to be functional, organised and fast.

Using this book, anybody with the most basic computer knowledge will be able to build a complete web site for personal or business use. The principles of successful site planning and structure are included - plus step-by-step instructions for the most common tasks involved.

There is also a special support web page solely for readers of this book at the address shown below. If there are any online tools or resources mentioned throughout the text, you will be able to find a direct link to them at this page. This is to ensure that you have the very best (and latest) information at your fingertips when creating your web site.

www.net-works.co.uk/create.htm

Chapter 1

Why Build A Web Site?

If you're curious enough to want to know how to create to web site, you've probably already made up your mind that you're going to build one. But why?

This may sound like a strange question, but there are actually quite a number of people that have built a personal or business web site just because they could. The end result is not unlike many home videos: a waste of time and effort that is of little interest to anybody (except maybe to its creator and their immediate family).

Why Build a Personal Site?

One of the greatest strengths of the web is also one of its greatest weaknesses: it provides the individual with an unprecedented power to publish. This can be especially useful to the world at large if the publisher has important or interesting information to impart, but only tends to clog up the web like so much pollution if the material is of no use or has already appeared in a thousand other places. Web pages that are mainly comprised of links to 'your favourite sites' are a good example of the former, teenage angst poetry being an excellent example of the latter.

Those who provide the most interesting or useful personal pages do so with a clear sense of purpose. They know enough and care enough about a particular subject or interest to publish individual material about it - much like writing a book, but a lot easier. Considering how useful you might find other web sites of this nature, perhaps you feel you might also want to publish a page or two of your own on a subject you feel strongly about or are well versed in. Think of it as giving something back to the web community.

Why Build Commercial (Business) Site?

In the past, you may have seen a few 'corporate' videos promoting one business or another. The best of these are short, have a central message and a core purpose - the worst are long, rambling and are a colossal waste of money. The same goes for web sites. You should only commit to a commercial web presence if it will be of direct benefit to your business - and the key to providing a benefit for yourself, is in enabling potential customers.

This consideration can vary from making your contact details easy to find, to supplying customers with valuable information, or even allowing them to do business with you directly over the Internet.

Yes, it is a two-way street, but the rewards for your business are clear:

- Being easier to find makes you accessible to more potential customers
- Streamlined communication improves efficiency
- Providing detailed information about your products reduces enquiry-related expenses and leads to more confident, 'self-educated' customers
- Supplying added-information of benefit to customers increases confidence and goodwill
- Linking all of this to an immediate transaction (or an easy way to enquire about your goods or services) increases the chances of sale closure and reduces the usual trading and/or marketing expenses

There are many cases of wonderful high-tech sites that have been built by large corporations - at great expense - that achieve none of these things. Similarly, there are also many business who have tackled the web with a clear agenda, only to be let down by poor delivery. (No matter how strong the purpose, if the site does not function as planned, all of your efforts will be wasted.)

In closing, before you learn about the how you must first be clear as to the why. Only once you have done this can you confidently move on to the practicalities of building the most effective web presence for this intended purpose.

Chapter 2

What You Need

A Computer
Well this one is kind of obvious, but we should explain that a PC is probably going to serve you better than a Mac in terms of getting the very best value out of the Internet.

For a start, most of the free software available on the Internet is for the PC, including many of the tools that can help you build a better web site.

An Internet Connection
Again, somewhat obvious, but if you want to receive enquiries directly from your site - and be able to change and update it yourself - then you will need an Internet connection.

You should also settle on a browser/email package that you are comfortable with. This type of software normally comes as standard with your connection, but it should be pointed out that the world's most popular browser is Internet Explorer. Since you will need to view your site as most of your customers see it, it is advisable to install this browser and use it to test your pages even if you don't plan on using it for your own web browsing.

Web Space
Web space is where your web site is kept. It is from here that it can be viewed by anybody from around the world 24 hours a day, 7 days a week. (Contrary to popular belief, your web site is not viewed directly from your computer, and you do NOT have to be connected to the Internet for people to view your web site.) Most ISPs - Internet Service Providers - include web space as part of your connection deal. The amount of space available to you can range anywhere from 2Mb to 20Mb, but most well-designed sites can fit into a mere 1Mb and still have room to spare.

If you do not have web space allocated to you as part of your connection agreement, then it may be time to consider changing ISPs. Alternatively, there are a number of 'virtual hosts' that will store your site for you. Many of these offer the service for free. Most of those that do charge for the privilege include a domain name in the deal.

A Domain Name
Well, this really isn't necessary - unless you think so. Not many people find sites by typing a company name and then '.com' (unless, of course your company is Coca-Cola). For the most part, domain names are only important in terms of company image. If you're an international company with an established name, then a domain name is a given. However, if you're a plumber with one van, no one is going to bat an eyelid if your web site address is http://www.ispname.com/joesplumbing

Authoring Software
Unless you're willing to learn HMTL from scratch, you are going to need an authoring program to help you build your pages. Basically, this kind of program makes creating web pages as easy as typing a document. There are a number of programs that do this, but the one we will be concentrating on in this book is Microsoft Word. This is not only because it includes very easy-to-use web authoring tools, but also because it is widely regarded to be the standard word processing format for offices around the world and many people are likely to already have this software on their computer.

Don't worry if you do not have Microsoft Word, as there are many other free web-authoring programs available for download, and they operate in much the same way. Latest versions of the two most popular web browsers - Internet Explorer and Netscape Communicator - also include web authoring programs with a very similar interface to that of Microsoft Word.

Graphics Software
The Internet is famous for its multimedia capabilities, so it would be foolish to ignore the most obvious feature of your page - graphics.

You may not think you need any pictures for your site, but it should be noted that a certain level of graphic design (i.e. company logo, navigation buttons, backgrounds etc.) is essential to good web design. Otherwise, all you are presenting is a page of text.

If you only plan on building a 'personal' page, then there are thousands of sites on the web that will be more than happy to offer you free graphics for your page. There are even some sites that can help you make individual images just for your page.

If, however, you plan on making a 'commercial' site, then you will most probably be required to pay for this kind of service. Alternatively, you may wish to make the graphics for yourself. If you already have a company logo and only plan on introducing this and a few lesser elements to your site, then you should be able to get by with a very basic graphics program. If there isn't one already on your computer, then there are many free products available for you to download.

Should you want to develop a logo or create special graphics for your site, then you will need a more advanced program. Also, if you want to include pictures of your products, you will need to invest in a digital camera (or a scanner to scan in printed photos). Happily, most hardware of this kind, (especially scanners) include free graphics software that should more than suit your needs.

A Level of Skill
We can show you the brush and how to use it, but the final result will depend a lot on your ability to make what is - in effect - a presentation document. In the end it pays to know your limitations and tailor the content of your site to your particular skills.

Knowledge
Step one is picking up a book much like this one. Along the way, you'll learn how to draft your content, introduce graphics to your concept and bring it all together in a basic web-authoring program. Before you do this, however, you need to spend some time on the web - not only to see some examples of good and bad sites, but also to gauge the best strategy for your particular application.

...Creating a Website

Chapter 3

Research

You may be tempted to dive right in and start building - but if you want your site to be successful and well travelled, then there are a few steps you will need to take first.

Number one is research, but don't worry, this can actually be a lot of fun.

If you've been on the web for some time, then you probably not only know your way around, but already have an idea of the kind of site you wish to make. Even if this is the case, it would still pay you to undertake some committed research regarding your project. You may end up seeing many sites in a whole new light.

Because the web evolves so fast, we have decided not to show any particular examples. For the same reason, listing any actual directories would be futile as something better could, and usually does, come along. Instead, we refer you to our support web page, which will have the latest links for you to follow regarding each and every section covered in this chapter. This method not only makes sure you have the latest information available, but also puts a large majority of your research needs a mere click away.

The Best Sites

High End Design
Many of the best sites are made by teams of well-funded design experts, armed with years of experience and the latest software. Nevertheless, this is one of the first places you should look, as even the professionals can get it wrong sometimes and there are important lessons to learn from this. For a start, some sites may look fantastic at first glance, but could very well be regarded as 'design-heavy' (in that they spend so much time trying to be beautiful that they cease to be functional). Also, a site that relies

heavily on graphics will take longer to load. Neither of these circumstances is particularly desirable, as a user who is new to the site may not wish to bother with a long download - and, if they do, they are unlikely to find what they want.

Professional Portals
Portal sites act as a browsable directory to the Internet, and as such they have a lot of information to organise. Watching how these sites achieve this can be extremely educational, especially as you'll see how many choose to do things in much the same way, while still managing an individual look. You will also notice that these sites use a minimal amount of graphics, as it is important to their users that the pages load as fast as possible.

Note - Many of these portals also have a 'cool' or 'latest sites' section, often featuring reviews to help you along.

Content Rich Sites
Again, these sites must be very well organised if they are to be effective to their users - but often the content involved requires large pictures and the like. Online newspapers and encyclopaedias are an excellent example of this and, for the most part, hold back on graphics as much as possible until the user gets to the section or listing they are particularly interested in. If a visual reference is required as part of the selection process, they will more often than not use 'thumbnails' (smaller, compressed versions of the picture involved).

The Worst Sites
OK, now we've depressed you with a series of sites you could never hope to emulate, it's time to have a little fun. Believe it or not, there are almost as many directories of bad sites as there are of good ones. Most of these deal with issues such as poor organisation and overblown design - usually from people who really should know better - i.e. the 'professionals'. If you want to see bad web sites made by amateurs, you won't have too look far. In fact you can probably start by browsing through some of the sites

hosted at 'free' servers such as www.geocities.com (while we did make mention of the ever-evolving web, there are some things that never change).

Common amateur mistakes include horrendous colour schemes, too many large graphics, backgrounds that take ages to load and don't let you read the text properly or too many 'bells & whistles' such as animations, sound effects and the like. This is an important part of your research if you plan on building a personal page, as these sites use many (often *too* many) of the free graphics and tools available to you. You will notice many of the 'extras' on these sites appear again and again and are, in the end, a waste of time.

Sites Relating to Yours

This is especially important to those wanting to build a site to promote their business, but can also be of benefit to those wishing to make a personal site. After all, there would be very little point in building your web site if there are thousands of others that cover exactly the same subject matter or interest(s).

The process is much the same for both applications - simply start at the search engine you are most comfortable with and experiment with a few words relating to the kind of site you wish to build. Make a note of every site that you are particularly impressed with, and those that you are not. Also bookmark the sites that turned up first in your search - it is these you should study closest, as they have managed just what you want to achieve and you need to ask yourself why this is the case.

For the most part, they will have used effective HTML tools known as 'META Tags' to ensure that those searching for their site can find them. You can see these hidden META Tags by selecting 'View' then 'Source' as shown. This will bring up the HTML code of the page. The META Tags, if they are there, will be easy to spot within the 'head' of the HTML code. In Chapter 9, we will show you step-by-step how to make and insert these important tools into your web pages. It sounds scary, but this is really the only HTML you need to deal with and we'll stick with you every step of the way.

The Net-Works Guide to...

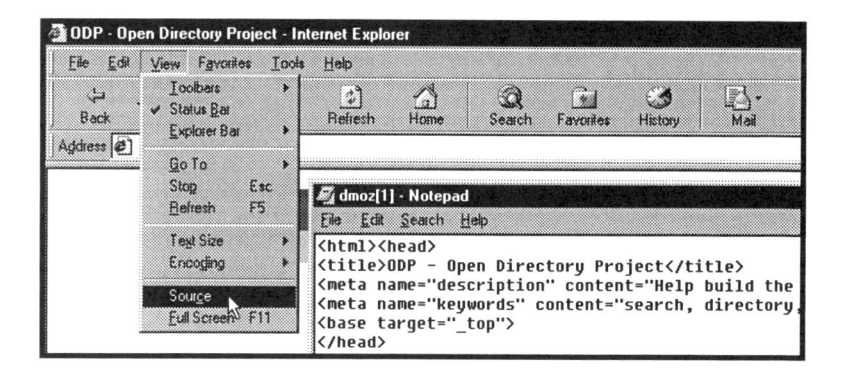

Another element that leads to these top results is site popularity, so you will also need to look at the content of the site and how it is presented to try and judge why this is one of the most popular of its kind.

Along the way, you may also find some directories specific to the subject matter of your planned site. You should bookmark these for future reference, as you will need to submit your site to these directories once it is finished.

For now, however, it's time to start thinking about the content of your site.

Chapter 4

Content

During your research, you will have noticed that many sites have a lot in common - in that while they may look different, many of them have more or less the same functionality. You too should adopt some or all of these common practices, as it is what your audience expects from a well-organised site.

It doesn't stop your site from being different; it just makes it user-friendlier. For instance, *Star Wars* is a very different movie from *Casablanca*, but they both have a beginning, a middle, and an end. Your site should be organised in such a way that new users have a clear idea of what is available - and also some common ground that they can rely on should they get lost or confused along the way.

This courtesy is just one of the many small touches that regular web-users appreciate. It will go a long way to making a good first impression.

Common elements that most sites share include the following:

A Navigation Bar

This is a series of buttons that not only let users know what the main areas of the site are, but also allows them to go to these sections with a click of the mouse. The navigation bar usually appears on the top or the left of the page - and should appear on every major page within your site. This is so visitors to your site can get to where they want to go with one or two clicks.

Even the largest and most complex sites try to keep their navigation bar as simple as possible, and always within reach. Often larger sites will use 'frames' to achieve this (frames allow users to scroll down one section of the site while the navigation bars remain static) but if you keep your pages brief and to the point this level of programming will not be necessary.

Aside from the selections regarding the individual purpose of the site, navigation bars are comprised of four common sections - with names that are largely universal. You should stick with these names wherever possible, as it provides the 'common ground' that users of your site will need to find their way around easily.

- Home
- About Us
- Links
- Contact

A 'Home' Page

Also known as the 'welcome' or 'index' page. It is this page that visitors to your site usually see first, so it should contain *at a glance* what the purpose of the site is and what the most important or interesting features are. You really want to put your best foot forward here, but at the same time you want to remain very selective and suitably restrained. Most of the web sites claiming to be the 'best', 'funniest' or 'most incredible' on the web are actually some of the worst, and you risk tarring yourself with the same brush if you use similar phrases. Also, if you put too much on the page, new visitors will not know where to look and your core message will get lost in the process.

For business users, one of the biggest issues on the web is trust, so you will find that a short testimonial from a customer is remarkably effective - particularly if the name below the quote has a link the user can follow to email the referee and verify their opinion. Virtually no one will do this of course, but the fact it is there will add considerable strength to the words. (Of course, if you take this measure, you will need the permission of the referee involved.)

If the contents of your site have changed, or if your business has a special offer, then you may wish to put these snippets of news on the home page as well. This is so visitors returning to your page can know immediately what is different about the site or service since they were last there.

The only thing you should *not* put on your welcoming page is anything like 'welcome to my/our web site'. This makes regular web users cringe, and will lose you a lot of credibility. How often do you see a TV commercial starting with "Hi, and welcome to the advertisement"?

An 'About Us' Page

Mostly this is only necessary for a business, and is where you would put a short history of the company and a list of the products/services you provide. Be brief, to the point - and above all, modest.

If you are building a personal page, it's probably best not to turn this into an 'About Me' page. This is often seen as being somewhat narcissistic, and is generally frowned upon by other web users - especially if it features a picture of you sitting in front of your computer!

Of course, if your site is about your amazing travels around the world, a personal campaign to free the Tasmanian tigers or your search for an original mint copy of Action Comics No1, then users may actually be interested in knowing why you do what you do.

A 'Links' Page

This is a series of links to web sites that visitors to your pages may find interesting or useful. For a personal page, this is limited only by your imagination, but try to make them as relevant as possible and avoid providing thousands of links to pages that everybody knows about already.

That said, your links page can also be a useful tool for you. If, for instance, you are at another computer besides your own (without your usual 'bookmarks' or 'favourites'), then you will simply be able to go to your web site and have all of your favourite sites at your fingertips.

For a business site, some more careful thinking is required. Of course you want to provide links to sites that are as relevant as possible to your business, but at the same time you don't want to send customers off to a competitor's site for obvious reasons. If you're a small business, then the answer is simple: a series of links to web sites of other small businesses in your area. If this is well organised and/or the only directory of its kind, you may well find increased site traffic as a result of this page.

Alternatively, you can supply a series of links to sites that educate users about the kind of product or service that you provide in an effort to make them a better-informed and/or more motivated customer.

If you do link to another site of equal standing to yours, then tell them. In general, it is considered polite for such links to be reciprocal, so it never hurts to ask (or at least hint politely). We reveal the importance of such links to your site in Chapter 12 when we discuss getting the best results out of search engines.

A 'Contact' Option

You'll notice we didn't use the word 'page'. Well, if the only point of contact you wish to have through the site is email (and there's only one email address that you wish to use) then why should you bother linking to a page that only has one link on it? It would be far simpler to put the link to your email address directly into this button!

Of course, a business site may be required to give more information and guidance.

For a start, rather than providing a straight email link, you may wish to use an online 'enquiry' form. This not only looks more professional, but also allows you to garner information from your prospective customer and put enquiries into a standard and easily recognisable format. This way you will instantly know which incoming emails are enquiries, and have the information you need to proceed with a quote or follow-up. Of course, users of the site will like to think that they have a choice in the matter, so you should include a straight email link along with the form. This is so users who wish to make a comment about your business or your site can do so without feeling that they are forced to make a formal enquiry.

Other information you include on the site is entirely up to you - but be aware that if anybody takes offence to the nature of your site then they may use this information for less than honourable reasons. If you have a business address - or especially a shop that you wish to encourage people to visit - then you should not only include the full address on your contact page, but also a simple map to make finding you as easy as possible. Similarly if you have a business phone number, then you should include this as well.

Be warned. Site owners who are new to the web have been known to inadvertently break the rules of 'Netiquette' either by sending out unsolicited email or posting an 'off-topic' announcement to a newsgroup about their site. Things like this may seem harmless enough, but there are web users that take great offence to this or that simply lack perspective. More likely, they could forward your details to other web users with no real details about their gripe, just that 'this guy is an idiot and here is his address/phone-number'. The end result is you getting rude phone calls at 4am. If you work from home or are hesitant to release such details to all and sundry, then don't do it. A good rule of thumb is that there shouldn't be anything within your site that you wouldn't want to appear on the front page a national newspaper - and this includes your school photo.

Core Page(s)

This is the centre of your site and the information that you want users to absorb and/or act upon. The naming, structure and content of this area can vary greatly from site to site.

In a personal site, for example, it could be a picture diary of your trip to the Andes, information about your cigarette packet collection, a list of bad jokes Grandpa used to tell around the fireplace - just about anything in fact.

A business site is most likely to feature details of their products or services. Prices, rates, details about individual packages or goods - any information you think would be helpful in motivating a visitor to your site to part with their hard-earned money.

You may even wish to make this process more immediate and enable users to buy your products or book your services directly through the site. In effect, your core pages can be anything from a brochure to a shop - or both.

For a political cause, the details of your policies would be within the 'About Us' section, but as the main objectives would be to either raise funds, support your campaign or get people to vote for you, then this would be the focus of your core pages.

Whatever the nature of your core pages, if there are more than five of them, or if the text or pictures involve large files, then there will need to be a separate list of contents within this section. If there are only a few sections in your core pages, then you may wish to introduce these options into your navigation bar. For the most part, however, it is often better to get users straight into the part of your site that matters most, *then* show them the options available - rather than confronting them with too much information up front.

This goes especially for products. You need to get the punters into the store, as they may see something they didn't know they wanted while they are there. If they were able to pick up the one product they wanted at the front door, then you certainly wouldn't make many 'impulse' sales along the way.

This element is known as 'secondary navigation', and should be just as well organised as your primary navigation bar. Put simply, you would need to organise your products (or services, or even jokes) into groups according to type. This allows the user of the site to go to the type of product they want, then select the single product that is best for them from the list provided. From here they can click on that product to see more information about it and/or purchase it.

A Generative Aspect

This is, in effect, your bait. Many of the people who need just your kind of product, service or information may not necessarily know that they are looking for it. It is your job to get into the heads of potential users of your site and try to imagine what they might be looking for on a day to day basis.

As mentioned before, small businesses can benefit from a local or otherwise specialised directory. Alternatively, it may pay to remember that the Internet is also largely about information and entertainment. With this is mind, you will be able to see the value of a plumber providing information regarding what emergency measures to take in case of a leak, while a lawyer could very well provide some free common-sense advice regarding his specific area of law.

You can see in these cases that if someone found this (free!) information and needed further help, then yours would most likely be the individual or organisation that they would contact. Not only because information about your service/product is only a click away, but also because you have gained their good faith by providing a free service that they have found useful.

With regards to entertainment, you need to be very careful - especially considering what we have already discussed regarding someone taking offence to your site. While it may be tempting for a builder to publish some of the bawdier jokes regarding his profession, it is unlikely to hold your company in good stead and can quite possibly do more harm than good.

An excellent example of a popular builder's site involves a man with a van. Having particular problems with a backfiring engine, he decided to install a camera in the back of his van to record images of pedestrians reacting to the sudden loud noise. The tone of the site is most apologetic - but of course he points out that if more people used his services, then he could afford to fix or replace the van.

He may get millions of visitors that are unlikely to use his services (mostly because they live on the opposite side of the globe) but nevertheless, the visitors that do come to his site have received something of value and go away happy. Due to the subsequent popularity of this section, the site is also well travelled and novel enough to be linked to by many other sites. This improves his standing in search engines considerably (see Chapter 12) and virtually ensures that he is the very top result when some searches for a builder in his area.

Once you have decided on the nature of your content, it is time to start planning your site. This, believe or not, is mostly done without the aid of a computer.

Chapter 5

Drafting Your Pages

You may think that plotting your web pages out on paper is a waste of time - but in truth this will *save* you time for a number of reasons.

Firstly, and most importantly, if it is your first attempt at web pages then you will more than likely be reluctant to make any changes once you have sweated over a page or two. This usually means that any mistakes you start with you will end up keeping, and many aspects of your web site will end up being compromised.

Also, it is very tempting when building in this way to add nifty gadgets and freebies that 'seemed like a good idea at the time'. As it's usually best to avoid such extras, taking away this temptation will help you to avoid a lot of these impulsive mistakes.

Finally, there is a lot of planning ahead that you will need to do in order to make the process of building and linking your pages as streamlined as possible. As we move on to collecting/building graphics and the making of your web pages you'll find out more about the benefits of such forward thinking.

The First Draft

This is going to be a mess of scribble on one page as you write down the basic components of your site. It could be the result of a brainstorm between you and a few colleagues, or a case of you locking yourself in the office with a large cup of coffee and no interruptions.

You should ideally consider the following:

- What kind of people do I want to attract to my web site?
- What am I going to offer to attract them to my site?
- Once they are there, what do I want them to do?

- How am I going to motivate them to do this?
- What do I hope to achieve by getting them to take this action?

If you get stuck at any stage, just go back to the last chapter and think about how you are going to address the basics such as the navigation bar, the 'home' page and such - which should be enough to get the juices flowing. Once you have done your first draft, it is time to take your messy sheet of paper and start typing.

The Text Draft

No matter how good your site looks, if the content does not serve its intended purpose then all of your efforts will have been wasted. This is why it's important to calmly sit in front of a word processor and type your content before you start building your pages. As you do this, a few more things may occur to you and the plan may change. This is fine - and just what the draft stage is for. The beautiful thing is that everything you type can be copied and pasted into your pages once you start building them.

You should restrict the quantity on each page to a maximum of 100 words in a style that is formal yet personable. As you write, it helps to remember that you are playing to an audience of one person with a very short attention span.

Once you have finished your text draft, print it out and grab the nearest red pen. There will be a lot of mistakes that you didn't spot on screen - and a lot of waffle that you may wish to strike out altogether. Once you have made these changes, it might even be an idea to print it out afresh and get someone else to cast an appraising eye over it.

The Sketch Draft

By now you should have a clear idea of the purpose of your site, and the content you will be using to achieve your objectives. You should also have settled on the titles for each section, how much text is involved, and what pictures may be necessary (if any).

Take a blank sheet of A4 paper and fold it in half. When visually designing your site it pays to try and keep as much as possible

The Net-Works Guide to...

---

in the upper half - especially for your navigation. This 'top half' is what your visitors will see on their screen without having to scroll down.

The type of site we are going to show you how to design will involve a logo in the upper right corner and a navigation bar on the left, very much like the drawing below.

Once you have a blank template you are happy with, make a few photocopies and start experimenting with the different sections of your site and how you are going to organise things such as secondary navigation, pictures and the like into your format, above right.

Now you not only know what is going into your site, but how it is all going to fit together. You should know how many pages you are going to have in your site and what order you are going to present them in. (You should also decide on file names for each page in advance as shown - each name being a single word in *lower case*.

...Creating a Website

You can name your pages anything you like, but the file name of the main/home page must be 'index'. More on this later.)

HOME	index
PRODUCTS	products
B. Stretchers	product01
B. Magnets	product02
E. Grease	product03
L/H Monkey Wr.	product04
L. Weights	product05
P. Wash	product06
S/Line	product07
S. Hooks	product08
S. Shifters	product09
ABOUT US	aboutus
CONTACT	contact
LINKS	links

You also have a clear idea of the graphics you are going to need, and this is going to help a lot - especially when you consider that you need to make your graphics before you start building your web pages.

Making a Special Web Site Folder

Before we even get to the graphics, there is one final task left in terms of organisation - the creation of your special web site folder. All of the *finished* work that appears on your web site (HTML pages, graphics, etc.) will have to be saved to this *single* folder.

The way HTML presents and organises web sites is by pointing to local files such as graphics and other pages. If any of these files are in different folders, the document will not be able to locate them, as they are no longer 'local' files. Simple, right?

Even if you don't understand how and why this works it pays to keep all of these elements in one folder, as it keeps your site organised and makes sure that you don't forget to send any graphics, pages, etc. to the server when you 'upload' your site. Note: It is possible to have other folders or directories in your web space, but this requires the use of 'relative' addressing which is beyond the scope of this book. .

Just as it is important that *every* element of your web site is saved to this folder, it is *equally* important not to put *anything* in this special folder unless it is part of the web site. There's no need to 'clean up as you go', but before you do upload your web site you should go through and relocate (or delete) any of the files that are not part of your finished product. If you don't do this, you may end up sending a bunch of useless data to the server - this is a waste of your connection time *and* your allocated web space.

Chapter 6

Writing For The Web

Before you draft your written content, you should be aware of a few things regarding the medium and the habits of web users themselves. For a start, nearly all of the visitors to your site will be reading from a computer screen. This alone slows reading time by about 25%, and after a while can really start to strain the eyes (especially if the web site is poorly designed and the text is difficult to read).

You should also be aware that web users have a notoriously short attention span, and are unlikely to want to wade through mountains of text to find what they want - especially when another site is only a click or two away. Add to this the value many web users place on their surfing time (including the cost of the call) and you actually run the risk of insulting them if you don't get to the point quickly and succinctly.

Research has also shown that web users scan rather than read even the briefest of web documents - picking out words, sentences or paragraphs that interest them. When doing this they will invariably keep an eye out for any large, bold or linked text to get them where they want to be just that little bit faster.

Linked text (text that includes a 'hyperlink' allowing the user jump to another page or site with a click) stands out in particular, not only because it is a different colour and underlined, but also because it is instantly recognisable by web users as the source of more information.

However, it is important to use restraint when inserting links, as having too many makes them harder to scan and therefore pointless. Be warned that this does not mean you should break up a large amount of text and link it page by page. Breaking up your information in an effort to make it seem shorter just makes it harder to read all in one go, and almost impossible to print.

The Net-Works Guide to...

So make it short. Really short. In fact, take what you would normally write for a printed version of your document and cut it by half - if not more. Also, be aware that most visitors are only going to give your text a brief overview. You should not try to force them to read the whole thing, as many will simply give up and go elsewhere. Instead, you should play to your audience by making your pages easier to scan and linked to relevant information only where necessary.

As you can see, we've waffled on for several paragraphs before getting to the point - and this would never do on a web site. Instead, the above information would be delivered in the following format, with the main point(s) being delivered immediately (if not within the header or title itself).

Writing Effective Web Copy

- **Keep it Short**
  Write at least 50% less text than you would normally use.

- **Make it Easy to Scan**
  Make key points easy to see by using strong headers and bold text (not Italics, which are hard to read on screen).

- **Use Links**
  Use a hyperlink when you mention another page or site that may be of use to the reader.

- **Make it Easy to Print**
  Don't break up a topic to make it seem shorter - this only makes it harder to read and print.

The above text is not only less than a quarter the length of our opening paragraphs, but also covers the main points quickly, simply and in order of their importance. Were more information required, the header could link to another page that covered the topic in more depth. In this way, you provide those who are interested in the information with easy access to it, but avoid confronting them with a mass of text immediately upon arrival.

Nothing annoys web users more than having to 'scroll' on a main or index page. They should be able to see everything on offer at a glance so they can get where they want to be quickly and easily.

Some Other Tips

Make It Easy to Read
Dark text, light background. In fact, don't even be tempted to stray from good old black on white unless you honestly feel it is pivotal to your design to do so. Similarly, the default for linked text is blue - you should stick to this colour scheme wherever possible, as it makes these useful tools immediately recognisable.

Make It Simple
Remember that you are writing for an international audience; English may very well be a second language for some of them. Some may also be younger or less erudite than your good self, so avoid complex platitudes and 'big' words that serve no discernible purpose. The previous sentence is an excellent example of what to avoid. ;-)

Make It Universal
Even if you only expect English-speaking visitors to your site, you should be aware that there are also some spelling discrepancies from region to region. For instance, even Microsoft got it wrong by naming the bookmark function of their browser 'Favorites'. Anybody living in Australia or the United Kingdom would think the correct spelling of this word to be 'favourites'. The fact that a popular piece of software exists to amend this one small anomaly is testament to how much these regional differences grate on some people. If you are playing to a global audience, be aware of this.

Make it Personable
Though you have a potential audience of millions, you are - at any one time - playing to an individual. The favoured style is simple

and informal - almost to the point of conversational. But be aware that if your site is intended to be a professional one, then there is a point where you can get too familiar, thus reducing your credibility.

Be Objective
A particular pet hate of web users is 'hype'. This goes especially for those wishing to transfer their copy straight from an existing brochure for a commercial site. Such material is not only going to have to be shortened, but also softened considerably. Those building personal pages should also be aware of the dangers of hype, so try not to blow your own horn too much lest you alienate your audience.

Back Your Claims, Link Elsewhere
If you can provide links to external sites that back up what you have to say or include short testimonials from customers/visitors complete with links to their email address, this will boost your credibility a great deal.

Get Organised
In a recent paper on the subject of web usability, one cooking site in particular was criticised for organising its recipes in order of their date of publication (instead of being arranged alphabetically, by key ingredients or something equally useful). This kind of laziness shows a complete disregard for those wishing to use a site, and is sure to drive away many visitors. The contents of your site should be presented in a way that makes the information it contains as ordered and accessible as possible.

Being Smart Isn't Clever
Using 'cute' headers, rather than straightforward and descriptive ones, only serves to confuse viewers of your page. Weak puns especially should be avoided, as they tend to annoy.

Humour Isn't Always Funny
Being personable and informal does not mean being boisterous and rude. While your copy shouldn't be too dry and boring, you

should keep your target audience in mind. Remember that even though they may have similar interests, many will have different educational and cultural differences to yourself and/or those around you. Use caution and try to be warm rather than hilarious.

Words and Pictures in Harmony
Images and text should work together to help tell your story. There should never be a picture without relevant text or a formal caption next to it, and you certainly shouldn't include pictures just to make your site pretty.

Chapter 7

Graphics

The good news for those building a personal web site is that there are millions of free graphics available on the web for you to use on your pages. There are also many sites that have 'live' software running, so you can have individual graphics such as navigation bars generated on the spot and save them to your computer with a click. Restraint should be shown here, but if you try to stick to your draft wherever possible it should be easy to avoid going overboard. Also, you should never take a graphic from a site unless you have the author's express permission (unless it is a site specifically offering free material for non-commercial use) - this goes for text content as well.

There will be a series of links to the best sources for such tools and materials on the support web page for this book. There will also be a series of links for business users to follow - as you are going to need a good graphics program to create your own images if you plan on building a commercial web site.

Happily, there are many free graphics programs available, and the one you choose in the end will be a matter of personal choice. Generally, it pays to pick the most popular option (this will be the one that has been downloaded most, and download-sites usually mark these 'most popular' choices clearly).

As mentioned in Chapter 1, if you need to invest in a digital camera or scanner to create pictures for your web pages, then a quality graphics program usually comes as part of the package. Alternatively, you may wish to make an investment in a top quality graphics program. This may bite into your wallet, but it will greatly increase the ability you have to make individual and quality images for your site. The best packages also come with free clip-art that you *are* allowed to use for your web pages.

...Creating a Website

The graphics software used for the following examples is a professional package called Corel Photo-Paint (while the industry standard is Adobe PhotoShop, it is best suited to a Macintosh computer and isn't quite as easy to use as Photo-Paint). Even though this is a professional program, the principles remain more or less the same - and many of the features and options you will see being used are also available with free programs.

Graphics Format

Any graphics you make for your web page are going to need to be saved in JPEG of GIF format. JPEGs are better for greyscale (as it compresses better) or for natural colours in photos (such as scenery or flesh tones).

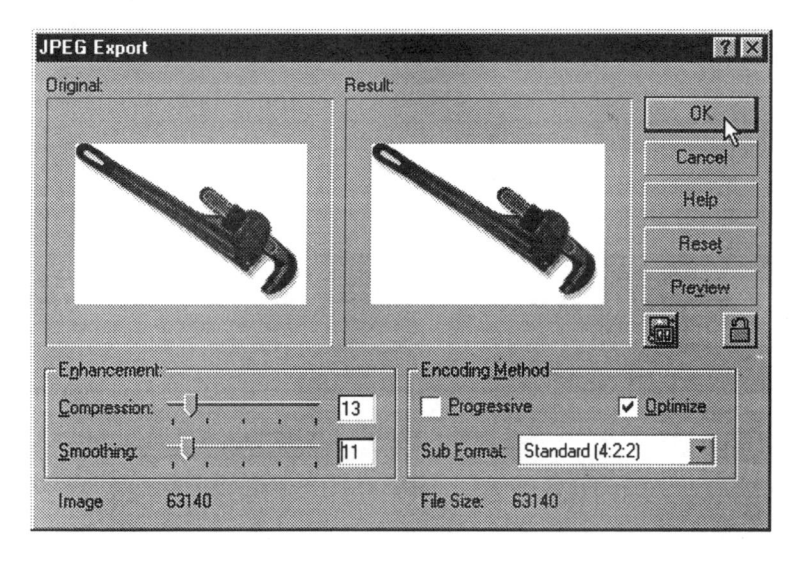

Saving a photo as a JPEG. Note the compression settings.

GIFs, on the other hand, are not only great for primary colours in logos, cartoons and the like, but also let you create effects such as transparent backgrounds (so not all of your images need to appear 'square').

With the right software, you can even bring together a collection of GIFs to create your own animations. There are many free and easy to use programs available for this, and you will find links to some of the best at our support web page.

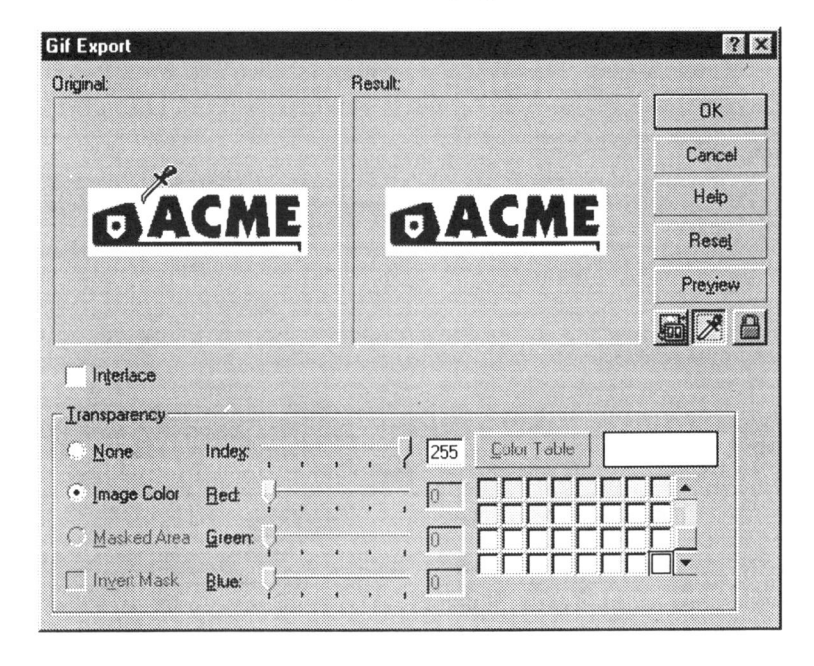

Saving artwork as a GIF and setting the 'transparent' colour.

Even the most basic of graphics programs will allow you to save a picture as a JPEG or a GIF, though not all will allow you to set the *resolution*.

Because your web pages are only going to be viewed on a computer screen, there really is no need to go beyond the maximum screen resolution of 72dpi (dots per inch). If you are an artist and wish people to be able to print wonderful images from your page, then you may wish to save these images at 300dpi - but everything else on your page should be at the *minimum* resolution so the file sizes are smaller and your pages *load faster*.

Graphics You May Need

Logo
If you have a regular printing company, then they probably already have a copy of this on their computer. A quick phone call should get you a copy on disk, and if you are on good terms with your printer they may even save it in the right resolution and format for you (i.e. as a JPEG or GIF at 72dpi). Alternatively, you can scan it into your computer from a brochure or letterhead and go from there. Be aware that while you want to make your logo as presentable as possible, you want it to load fast so visitors to your site don't have to wait for it. The *maximum* file size for a logo should be around 10 kilobytes (10Kb).

Navigation Bar/Buttons
There are a number of ways you can present the major links in your navigation bar, but as these are the main links to follow in the site, they really should be graphics rather than straight 'text'. This not only makes them stand out from the written content, but also helps you create a more elegant 'look' for your site - especially if you take the time to make sure they compliment your logo or other artwork. Again, you should be careful to make the file sizes of these graphics as small as possible, as you do not want users of your site waiting around for these very important elements. Ideally, each bar or button should be no more than one or two kilobytes in size.

Pictures
Try and trim the pictures you wish to present. If there is a single product you wish to sell, then your focus should be the product (not the background). Similarly, if you wish to show a picture of your dog (we really wish you wouldn't, but if you absolutely must) then you should trim the picture to show the dog, and not the great big hedge he is standing in front of. Again, an absolute maximum file size of 10Kb. If you need to have larger graphics than this (say, examples of your artwork), then it's thumbnail time.

Thumbnails

Thumbnails are reduced 'samples' of larger pictures. As mentioned earlier, this comes in very handy when a visual guide is required as part of the selection process. For instance, if you wanted to show an index of the beautiful photos you have taken, you wouldn't get very far with text ('beach at sunset', different beach at sunset' and so on). Often a thumbnail is more descriptive than words will ever be. The thumbnail method can also be used to provide 'previews' of products that can be viewed in full if your visitor wishes to do so.

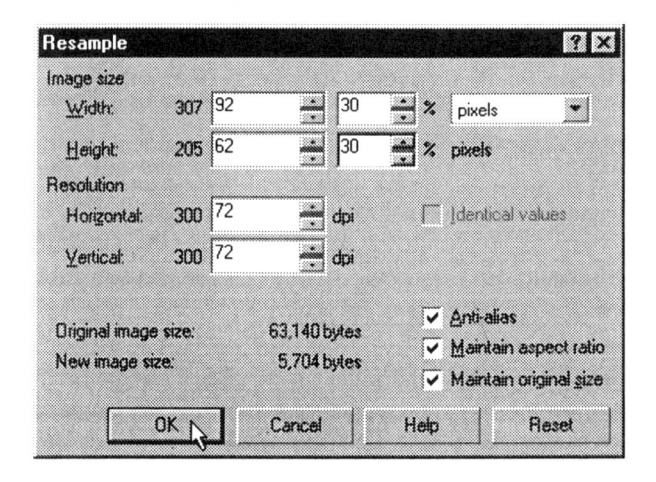

A typical set of 'resample' options that allow you to reduce the resolution and/or dimensions of a picture. In this case we have reduced the picture to 30% of its original dimensions and reduced the resolution from 300dpi to 72dpi. Note the greatly decreased file size, which has plummeted from over 60Kb to under 5Kb.

Some Hints and Tips

Creating at High Resolution
Though you want to save the final result at 72dpi, it pays to create original artwork in a document set to 300dpi, especially if you are planning on a great deal of image manipulation (rotating objects,

changing colours etc.). The reason for this is that if you rotate or change any object within a document set to a lower resolution, a compromise will have to be made with each change as the computer tries its best to represent the altered image. Really, all image creation and editing should be in a high-resolution environment. Once you have a finished image you are happy with, you can then reduce the resolution.

Planning a Good Navigation Bar

When creating graphics for your navigation bar, it pays to think ahead. If you plan on running your bar across the top of your page, the total width of all of the buttons involved should not exceed the ideal page width (this is just under 800 pixels - more about this later). If you plan on running your navigation table down the left (as we will be teaching you how to do), then you will need to start with the button with the *longest* name first. This is to make sure that you can effectively set the maximum width of your navigation bar - and not end up creating a bunch of wonderful graphics only to discover that one of your buttons is just too darn long! The maximum width of left-orientated navigation buttons varies, but ideally it should be no more than 1/5 of your ideal page width (i.e. around 150 pixels).

Less is More

It pays to know the limitations of your abilities - and that of your graphics software. Above all, don't get carried away with flashy effects. The graphics on your site should be simple, stylish and in keeping with the theme of your page and/or corporate image. Also, be careful that any 'text' graphics you include are *easy to read*.

Repeat, Repeat, Repeat

Most browsers are set to save images they have already downloaded in a special temporary folder known as a 'cache'. This is so that when the user returns to the site, they do not have to download the same graphics all over again. For this reason, the smart web designer will repeat images such as navigation buttons, logos etc. - not only to give their web site a level of conformity, but also to make each page in the site after the first one load that little bit faster. This technique also makes building multiple pages for your site that much easier, as once you settle on a single 'template', you can quickly and easily create more pages from it.

Chapter 8

Making Your Template

For a start, it simply doesn't make sense to build twenty separate pages from scratch when you can quite easily make one blank or 'template' to start with, then save this as a set of multiple pages. Also, you are going to need to tinker with a few things before you get a look that you are happy with. You don't want to have to make these little changes across a large number of pages.

This is why it makes sense to start on (and experiment with) a single template until you are completely satisfied with the 'look' you have created, and are sure that all of the elements of your web site will fit within this template.

Let's Start Building
To create a new HTML document in Word, simply open the program and select 'New' from the 'File' menu as shown.

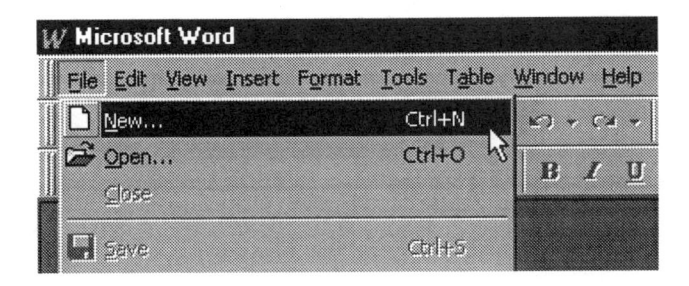

You will be given a series of options as to the type of new document you would like to create. If you have opted for the full installation of Microsoft Word, then there will be a tab on the far right titled 'Web Pages'. Click this, select 'Blank Web Page', then click 'OK'.

The Net-Works Guide to...

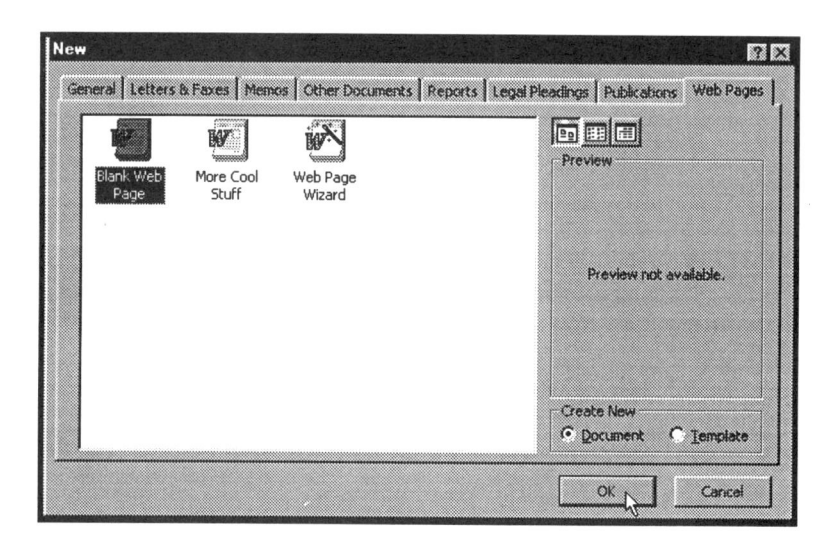

Note - If you are not presented with the 'Web Pages' option, then you have not opted for the full installation for Microsoft Word. If this is the case, you can easily install this extra facility from the product CD-Rom, or download the free HTML editing plug-in from Microsoft, or any of the many free download sites listed at our support page.

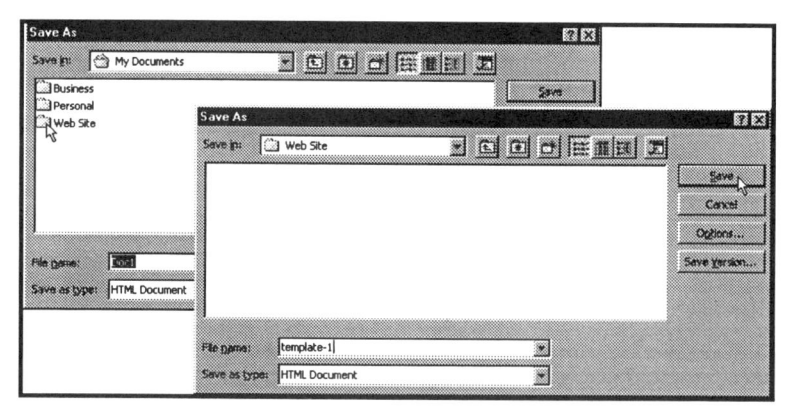

Before you do anything to your page, you are going to have to save it into your special web site folder. Select 'Save' from the

'File' menu (or just click the button that looks like a floppy disk). Go to your special web site folder and save your new document as 'template1' or something similar, see opposite.

Tables

The page we are going to show you how to build is of a standard design, with a navigation bar down the left. To separate your navigation bar from the rest of your content, you are going to have to create a 'table'.

It is important to realise when creating your table that different people have different monitor settings, the minimum of which is 600 pixels wide. This is why, when Word creates your table, it is 590 pixels in width.

However, the majority of web users have their screen resolution set at 800 pixels wide. This is generally regarded as the industry standard, so we are also going to show you how to change this and a few other properties of your tables.

Other users may have their monitors set to an even wider resolution, but if you keep everything within your table, it will still look nice and neat.

Note - If you do set your table width to over 600 pixels wide, those who wish to do a print-out of the web page will have to do so on the 'landscape' setting rather than the default 'portrait' setting (as your table will be wider than a standard A4 page). This is a minor concern if you don't really intend users to print your pages, but if your pages are designed for print-out, then you may wish to keep the default table width and work within that.

Creating a Table

Click the 'Table' button as shown and drag the mouse across a set of 4 cells (2x2). Click again and your table will appear.

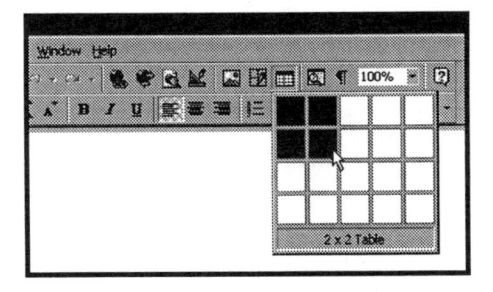

The Net-Works Guide to...

Changing Your Table - A Quick HTML Adventure

As we said, Word creates tables at just under 600 pixels wide. If you want to change this, you are going to have to delve into the HTML. This is actually very easy, as there isn't much code there at the moment, and the part you have to change is very easy to spot.

Consider this a quick training exercise for some HTML tricks we are going to show you later.

First, you will have to 'Save' your document (Word will not let you go into - or out of - the HTML editor without saving any changes you have made). Select the 'View' pull-down menu and click 'HTML Source'.

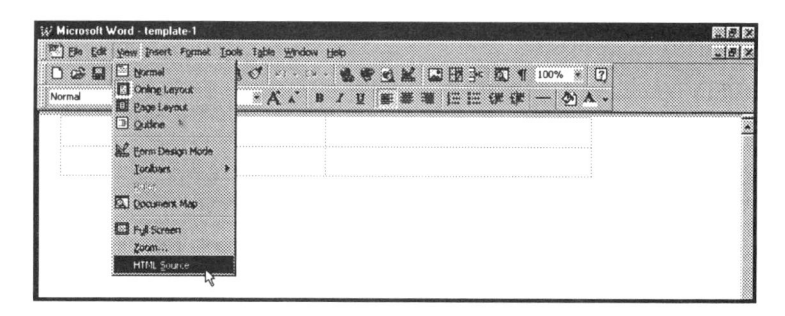

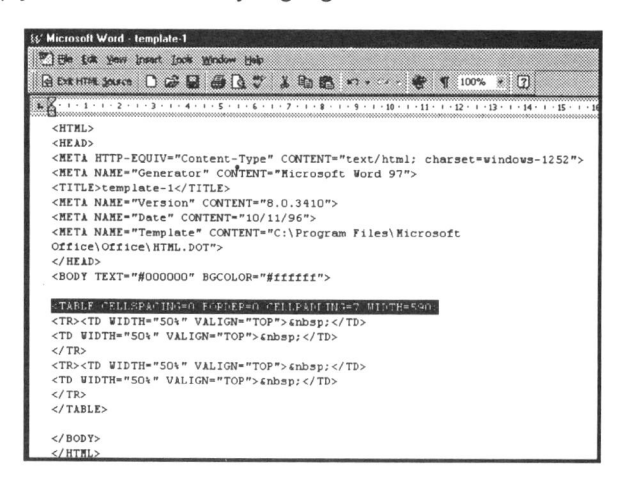

This will open the HTML of your document as shown with the part(s) you need to modify highlighted. To alter the width of the table, just change the value of the 'width' from WIDTH=590 to WIDTH=750. You may also note that the value of 'cellpadding' is set at 7, changing this to CELLPADDING=10 will give your text more 'elbow room' and make your pages look a lot neater - this is the space between your text and the borders of the table

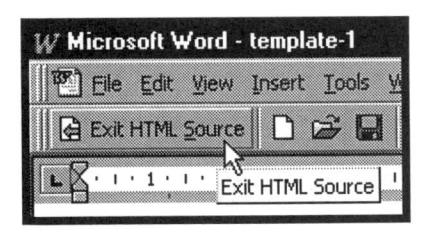

Once you have finished, click 'Save', then 'Exit HTML Source' shown.

Some Easier Changes

Resizing Cells
Once you come out of the HTML, you will see that the table now fills much more of the page. The next step will be to change the left column width for your left navigation bar (which, if you remember, should be about 1/5 the total width of the page). This is quick and easy to do. You start by mousing over the middle 'border' until the special cursor appears as shown. Click down and drag it to the left - it doesn't have to be exact, as you will need to adjust this width slightly when you add the graphics for your navigation bar.

The Net-Works Guide to...

Merging Cells

The top half of this table is going to be for the main part of your web site, the bottom is for all those extras such as copyright notices, counters and the like. You'll only need one single width for this, so you need to merge these two cells. Put the cursor in the bottom left cell, then click down on it and drag the mouse across the two cells until it is highlighted as shown. Select the 'Table' pull-down menu and click on 'Merge Cells'.

Changing Cell Colours

If you want your navigation bar to stand out, you can give it a block colour background. To do this, just put the cursor in the top left cell as shown and select 'Cell properties' from the 'Tables' pull-down menu.

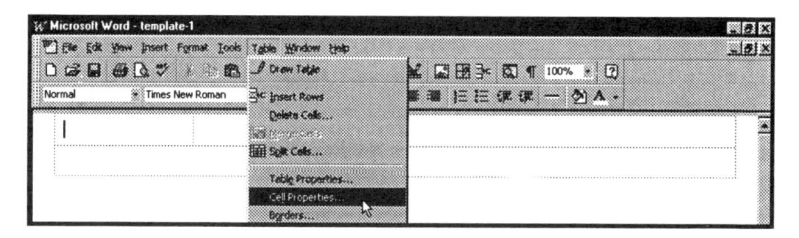

The box, opposite top, will appear, giving you a selection of primary colours to choose from. Choose one, then click 'OK' to make the changes and close the box.

If you like, you can choose to make the background of your navigation bars the same colour as the one you have chosen for this cell (black being the easiest). Alternatively, you can save your navigation bars as GIFs with transparent backgrounds. Either of these methods will give you a clean and clear navigation bar,

...Creating a Website

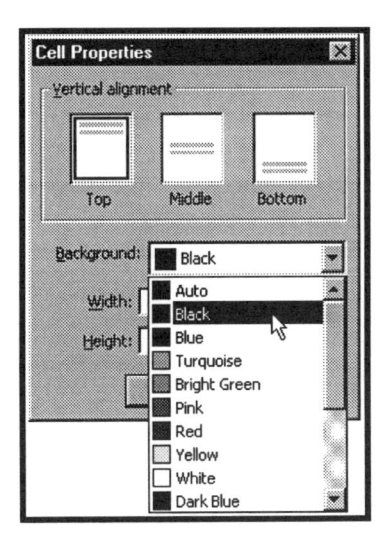

though you may need to experiment a bit as you introduce your graphics and your template starts to come together.

Graphics

Inserting Graphics
Inserting graphics is quick and simple. Just put the cursor where you want the graphic, then click the button that looks like a little

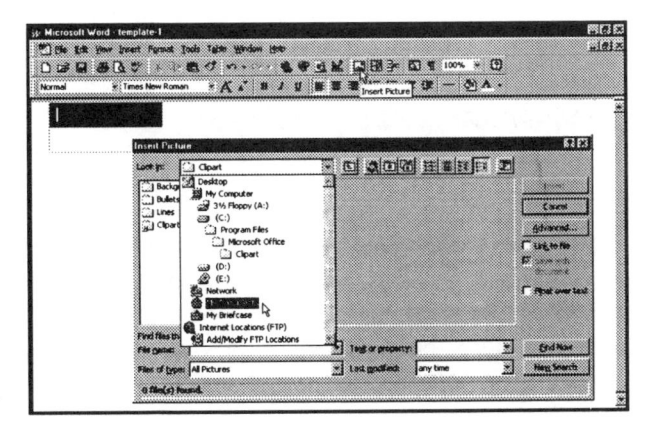

picture. The first time you do this, it will point to the 'Clipart' folder of Word, but it should be quite easy to locate your special web site folder from the pull-down window as shown on the previous page.

Once you are inside your special web site folder, choose the graphic that you wish to put in (in this case the first navigation button) highlight it, then click 'Insert'. As you can see, putting some thought into the names of these graphics, and a simple number after each navigation bar to show which order they go in, can make this stage so much easier.

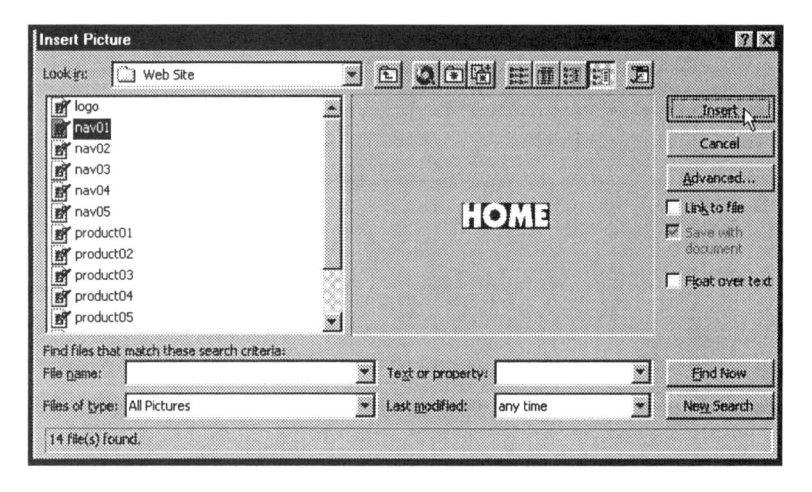

You will see that your button has appeared, and the cursor is flashing next to it. Hit the 'Return' key on your keyboard once, so the cursor appears below this first graphic, then insert the your next navigation button and continue until they are all in place, see top opposite.

Now you've made a few changes, a 'Save' of the document is well overdue. In fact, you should get into the habit of clicking 'Save' every time you make a major change to your document. This will save you a lot of heartache.

You can see here that the cell width we have set is ideal, but if it is too wide or too narrow, it is a simple matter to grab

...Creating a Website

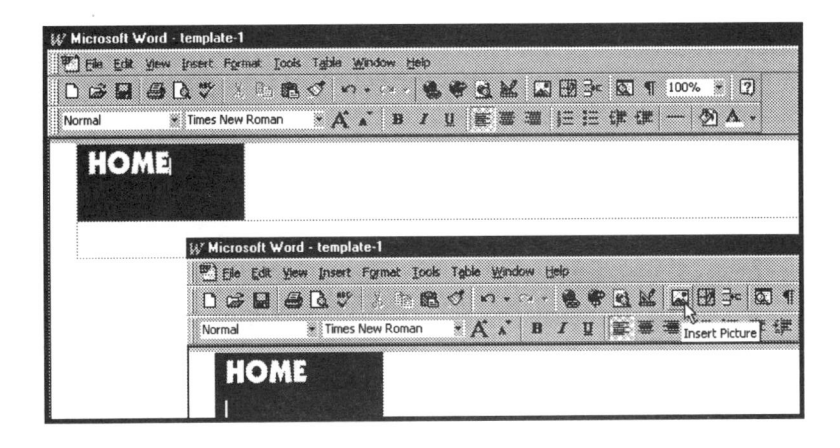

and drag the middle border to a better position. The next step is introducing **'alternative text'** for your graphics. This is very important, especially in the case of navigational graphics such as these. Alternative text are the words that appear before the picture loads, or when it fails to load for some reason. By assigning

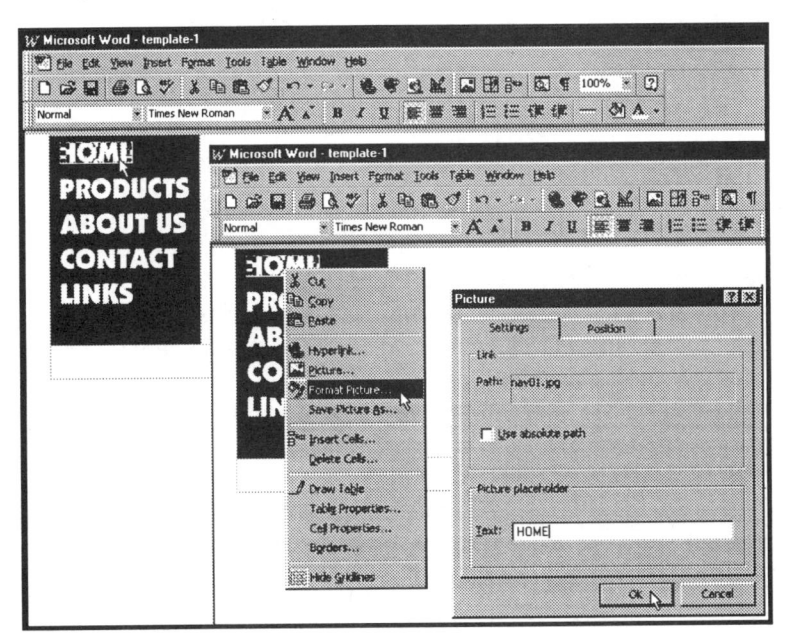

47

alternative text to a graphic, you are ensuring that those visiting your site will always know what the purpose of a graphic is, even if it does not appear.

To assign alternative text, just click once on a graphic until it is highlighted, then right-click. Select 'Format Picture' from the options provided. In the box that appears click the 'Settings' tab, enter the text that you want under 'Picture Placeholder', then click 'OK', see previous page).

To change the alignment (left, right or centre) of a picture, just insert as normal, highlight it and use the alignment tools as shown. In this case we have inserted the logo at the top right of the document. It is just under this, also on the right, that we are going to put the title of the page.

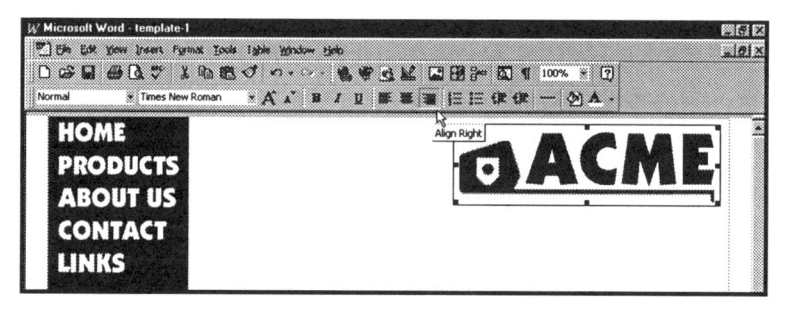

Text

You really won't need much help with this, as it's as simple as typing. In fact, many HTML authoring programs try to make it harder than it needs to be, and Word is no exception.

You shouldn't need to use many of the controls shown on the text tool bar shown below, but you should avoid the one on the far left especially. This tool is designed to create 'special' text such as headers and the like, but all it ends up doing is creating a bunch of unnecessary HTML commands that clog up your document, making it slower to load.

If you want to make text more prominent, it is a simple matter to make it larger or 'Bold' with the other tools provided. Let's show you an example in the next stage of our template.

...Creating a Website

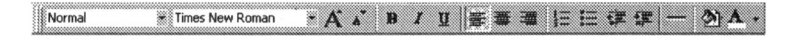

Type the word 'HEADER' in high caps as shown, then press the 'Return' key on your keyboard. In the line under type 'Sub Header', and in the line under that just write some text to fill.

If you want to change the alignment of text, just highlight the text as shown and use left, centre, or right alignment button.

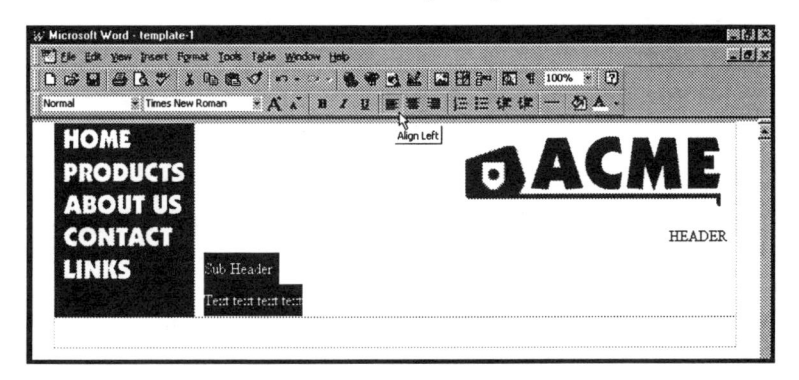

Highlight the 'HEADER' text and click on the 'Increase Font Size' button two or three times as shown, then click the 'Bold' button once.

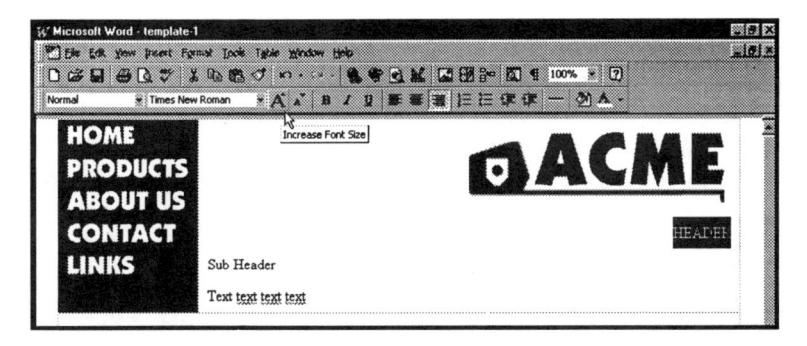

Then highlight the Sub Header, 'Increase Font Size' by one click, then make it 'Bold' too, see overleaf.

As you can see, this is all quite straightforward - but we're going to warn you again not to get carried away. While the tool on the

The Net-Works Guide to...

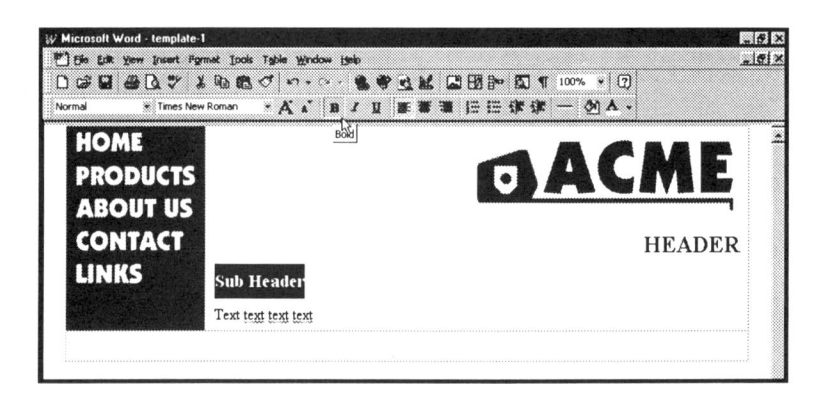

far right of the text control bar will allow to change text colour quite easily, we would advise that you stick with black text on a *white* or *very light* background. Being able to design a beautiful page while keeping your text clean and clear is a hallmark of good design.

Besides, just about all of us are used to reading in this universal colour scheme - over a billion books can't be wrong!

Similarly, there are a number of reasons to stick with the default font 'Times New Roman'. For a start, it's easy to read (and most newspapers in the world seem to agree). Secondly, the font you choose may not be installed on the computer of some visitors to your site. If this is the case, the computer picks the closest font it can find and displays that instead - often with disastrous visual results. The only reason you should depart from 'Times New Roman' is if you need a more modern look. If this is the case, then 'Arial' is also widely accepted and should be quite safe to use.

You template is now just about ready, but you may wish to tweak it around a bit, and maybe even use it to make a quick mock up of your busiest page to make sure everything fits. Often you may have to go back to square one on a graphic (or even a whole set of graphics), but making sure you get it right at this stage is going to make your life a lot easier.

You should also add the 'fine print' to the bottom all of your pages at this stage, as this way it will automatically appear on every page you make. The fine print is usually comprised of the specifics of the site ('this site best viewed with Microsoft Explorer at

800 x 600 resolution') and any notation of authorship or copyright you wish to include.

As you tinker with the page(s) to try and get the 'look' right, it pays to view the results occasionally via a web browser (preferably

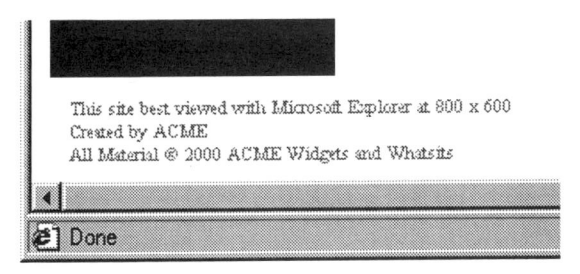

Internet Explorer). You can do this quickly and easily by selecting 'Web Page Preview' from the 'File' menu as shown.

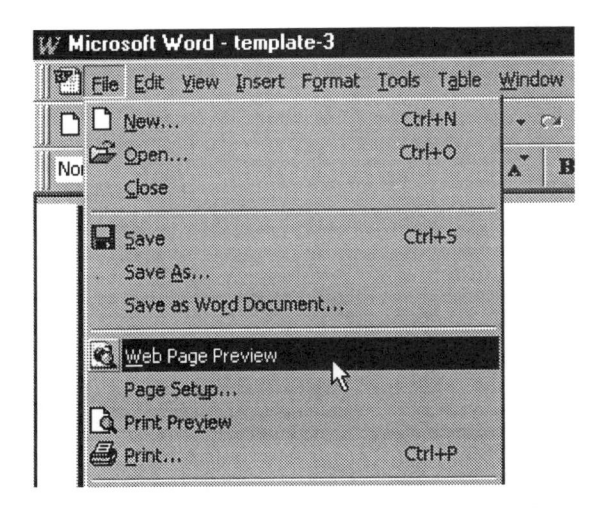

This will open the page you are editing in a browser window to let you see (more or less) how it will look for the folks online. Once you are confident in the look of your template, it's time to start

making a few links. This will be the first step towards making a multi-page site from your template, below.

Chapter 9

Making Your Site

The difference between a web page and a web site is quite simple. A web page is a single HTML document, while a web site is a series of connected HTML pages working together.

Hyperlinks

Hyperlinks (known commonly as 'links') are what turns your series of single pages into an interconnected site. They also allow you to link to just about any other web site on the World Wide Web and a lot more.
The three most common kinds of links are:

Local Links

A local link is one to another document or file at your web space (or, when viewing offline, in your special web site folder). All you really have to do here is point the link to a file name and it will automatically locate it and open it.

index.htm

External Links

With an external link, you will need to also provide information about the location of the file you wish to point to. This usually takes the form of a URL:

http://www.domain.com/index.htm

Mail Links

These work a little differently in that rather than pointing to another file, they open up a blank email in the visitors usual mail program that is pre-addressed to you (or another email address of your choice).

mailto:name@isp.com

Inserting a Link

To insert a Hyperlink into a graphic or text, you simply need to highlight it and then click the 'Insert Hyperlink' button as shown. In the 'Link to file or URL' box that will appear, enter the path to (or the name of) the file you want to link to and click 'OK'.

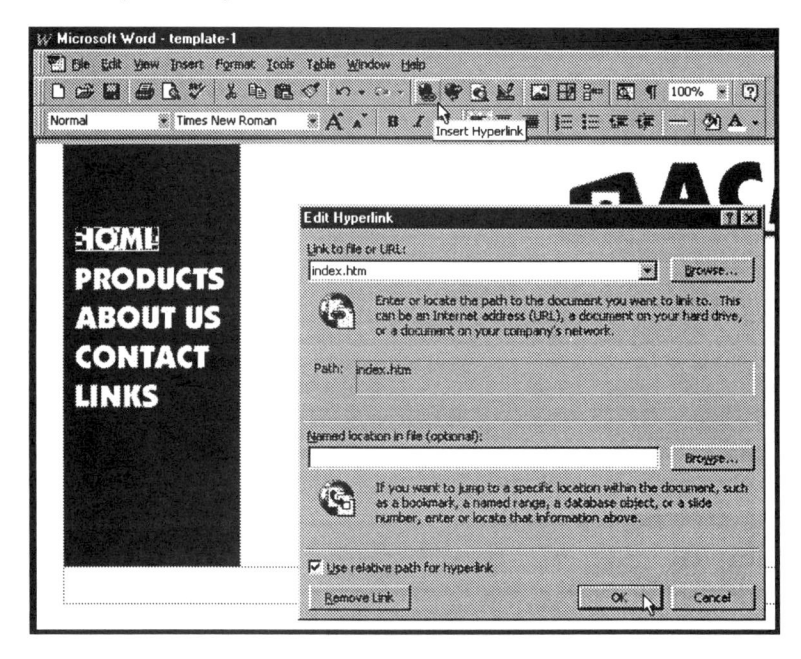

Now you're going to use this kind of link to make the navigation bar active. This is where your forward planning is about to pay off.

Highlight the first of your navigation bars (such as 'HOME' shown previously) and click the Hyperlink button. In the box that appears, type the name of the page you want this to point to, followed by '.htm'. (The '.htm' indicates the kind of file you are pointing to, in this case an HTML document.)

Because the home page is the main page (i.e. the page we want users to see first when they visit our site) you will be pointing this link to 'index.htm'.

Repeat this step for the other navigation buttons, referring to the file names you have decided on for each of the main

...Creating a Website

pages. Remember that though you may be linking to pages that don't exist yet, that this is why you have made a list of file names for each page that you are going to create- and they are going to exist very soon.

By now you are happy with the look of your template and all of the major links are in place. From here on, things get a lot easier.

What we're going to do now is go to your list of file names and make multiple pages out of your template. This will turn your single page into a web site that is virtually ready to go.

Open your main template and select 'Save As' from the 'File' menu.

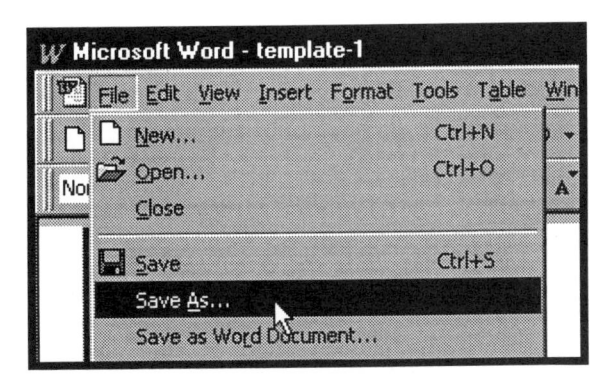

Save it into your special web site folder with the name 'index'.

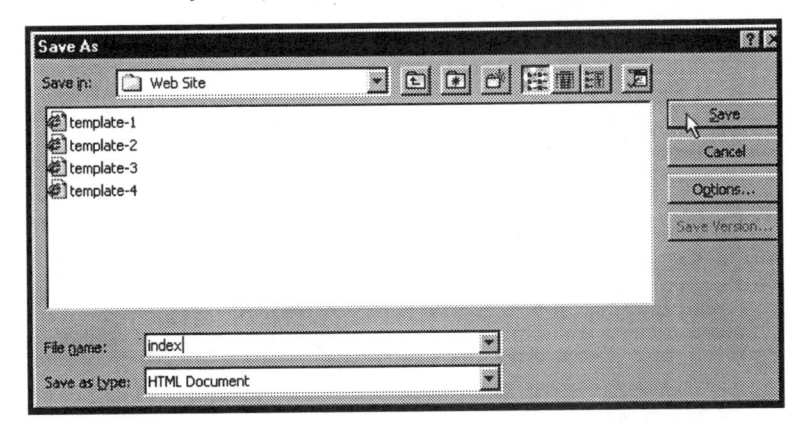

Repeat this process with your other file names until all of your pages are created. All you'll need to do now is open each of these documents in turn, paste in the text you have already written and insert any extra graphics as necessary.

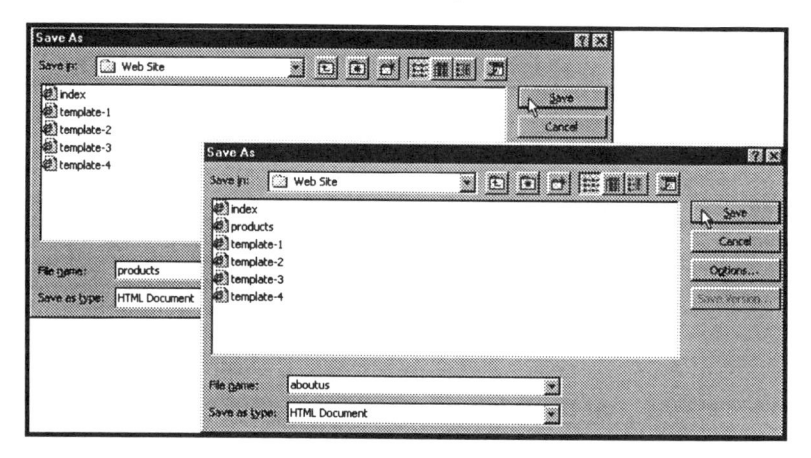

As you go along, remember to *save often* and open your documents in the web browser to preview them. This time around, you will not only be able to see how they will look online, but also test your local links and jump from page to page.

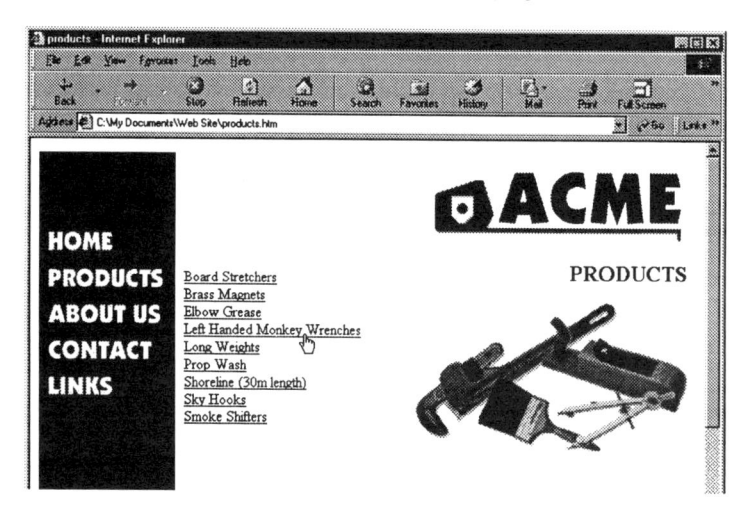

Chapter 10

Checking Your Site

Once your site is 'finished', it is time for the most important process of all - quality control.

You want to check your site thoroughly 'offline' before you put it live to the server; not only to check that it is *functional*, but also that it is *correct*.

Local Links

The first and easiest exercise is to check the 'navigation' of your web site. In other words, you need to check that all of the pages within your site are correctly linked so visitors can find their way around. Clicking on these 'local' links should take you from page to page just like any 'live' web site (the difference here is you are viewing your page from a location on your computer, rather than from the Internet). If any of the links are incorrect, you will have to go back into your HTML documents and check that the file names you are pointing to are correct.

Email Links

When you mouse over the email links, you will see that the related email address appears in the lower left of your browser. Clicking on these links should open a pre-addressed email - you can check this very quickly by sending it off with a 'Testing' subject header, though you will have to connect to the Internet to do so. The test email should arrive safely in your Inbox almost immediately. If not, you will have to go back into your HTML

> **Hint - If you've made a dreadful mistake and the same link on every page is pointing to the wrong file name, you may consider just changing the name of the 'target' file.**

The Net-Works Guide to...

document and check that the email address you have entered is correct and complete.

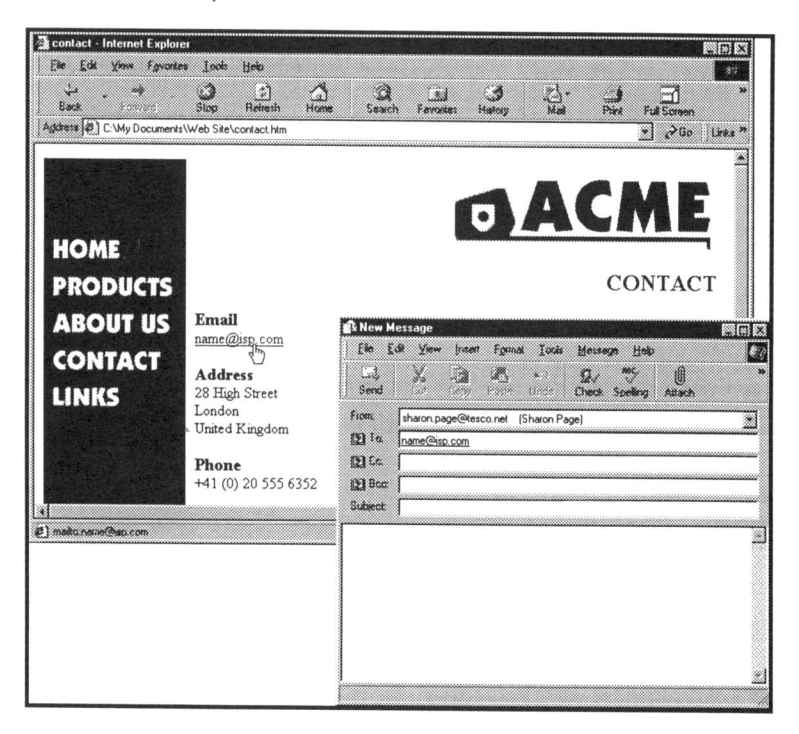

If a pre-addressed email fails to appear, it is most likely that you have forgotten to add the 'mailto:' command to your hyperlink in front of the email address. Another common mistake here is to put a space between the 'mailto:' and the email address - just to clarify, there *shouldn't be one*.

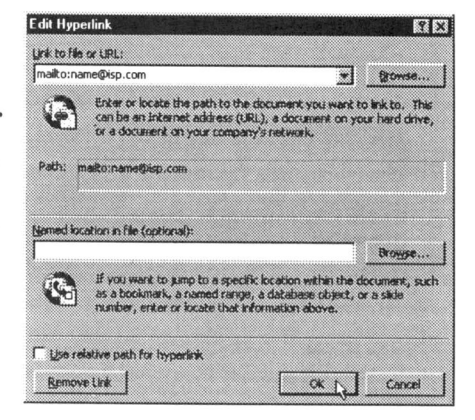

Online Links

Even though you are viewing your web site 'offline' you will be able to check links to other sites if you connect to the Internet. (As the information contained in these pages is stored elsewhere, your computer will have to be 'online' to access the information from the relevant servers.)

If the pages fail to load, or the link takes you to the wrong location, you will have to go back into the HTML document involved and check that the web addresses (URLs) you have entered are correct and complete. Usually mistakes here involve a simple typing mistake, but another common error is to forget to add the 'http://' before the URL.

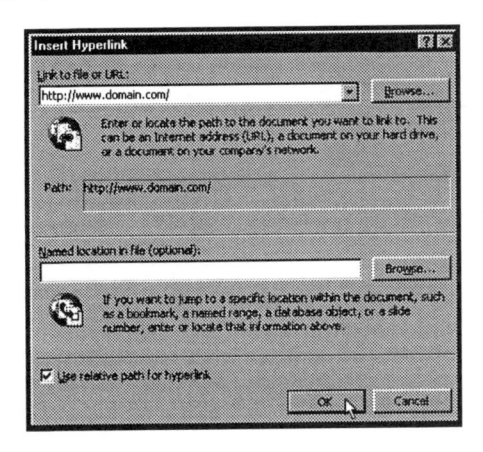

Graphics

All of your pictures should load without a problem, as you are viewing them directly from your computer. If any pictures do fail to load, it's usually the result of renaming or replacing a graphic file in your web site folder, but not telling your HTML page what the new file name is. You can fix this by reverting to the file's original name, or going back into the HTML document and re-inserting the graphic under its new name. Nothe that capitals are important when naming files and images; so Picture.gif is different from all of these:

- picture.gif
- Picture.GIF
- PICTURE.GIF
- Picture.Gif

Text
Check your *spelling*, check your *facts*! This counts for so much, especially if your web site is meant to be a reference tool. Also, if it is a business site, you are unlikely to make the right impression on potential customers or clients if it is full of spelling mistakes.

Getting Others to Check Your Page
It is a good idea to get someone else to check your web pages, as you will no doubt look past many mistakes - especially if you have looked at the same page dozens of times. It's surprising how often otherwise obvious mistakes get missed in this way, so it pays to have your web site checked by a friend or colleague before you upload it.

Print it Out
Doing print-outs of your web pages via the browser is a very good idea regardless of who you show it to, as often what looks good

on the screen will come out all wrong on the printer. For a start, most browsers are set to print web pages without background images or colours. This, combined with elements such as GIFs with transparent backgrounds and table widths, (see Chapter 7) can make your page a real mess upon printing. You shouldn't obsess over this (unless there are pages specifically intended for printing, like scripts, stories etc.) but you should at least be aware of it.

To print your web pages, just preview them as normal in the browser and select 'Print' from the 'File menu.

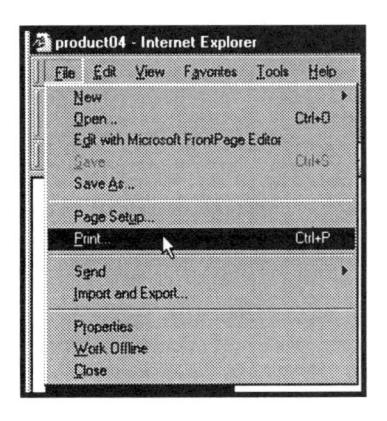

Save it to Disk

You can also copy your special web site folder to a floppy disk. Anyone with another PC will be able to open the folder, double-click in the 'index', then view your pages from this floppy disk. To copy your folder on to a floppy disk, just right-click on it and select '3 1/2 Floppy' from the 'Send To' options. While you're there, it may also pay to make a quick 'back up' copy for yourself.

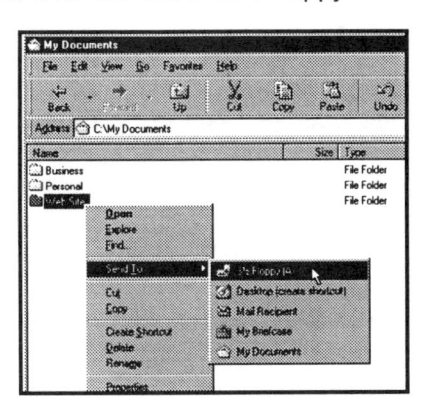

Chapter 11

Final Touches

As useful as a web authoring package is (like 'Word'), often some professional touches are not catered for and have to be done the old fashioned way. You'll remember earlier that we did a little fiddling in the HTML of a document. We're about to go back in and add two vital elements to the 'HEAD' of your HTML - the page title and some very important META Tags.

If you haven't already made a complete 'back up' of your web site, then now is the time to do so. Altering the HTML isn't that complicated, but often small mistakes in this area can have dire consequences.

Changing the Page Title

You may have noticed when viewing your pages through the browser that the titles of these pages were simple file names. You undoubtedly would also have seen some sites on the web with the page title 'index', 'Untitled Document' or similar; this often results from people either neglecting to change the page title, or being unable to.

We're going to show you how to change this as a warm up to altering your headers, and also to make your page look more professional.

Start by opening your 'index' page in Word, then select the 'View' pull-down menu and click 'HTML Source'.

This will open the HTML code of your document. You'll see the 'index' text in between the open and close of the TITLE code. Simply replace this text with a

...Creating a Website

better title (being very careful not to change the code around it), save your changes then click 'Exit HTML Source' as shown.

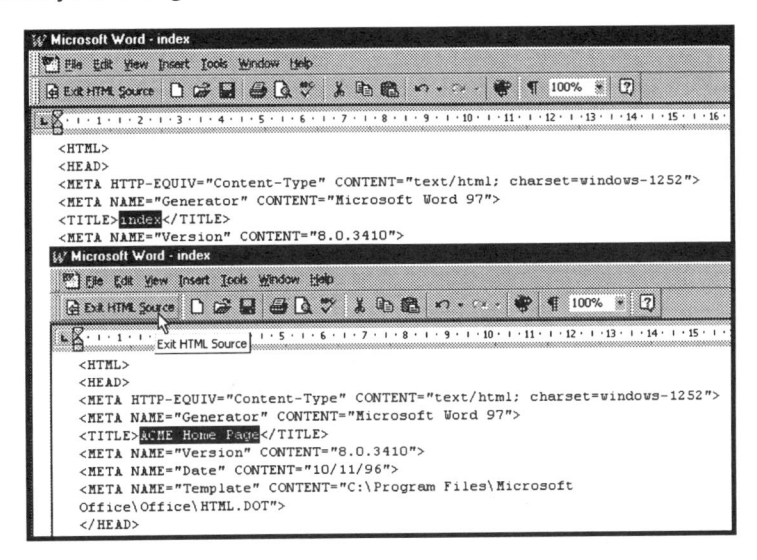

Now when you open your web page in a browser you will see that it has a much more descriptive title. (If it doesn't, try clicking the 'Reload' button on the toolbar.)

You have just successfully altered your HTML header. The bad news is that you are going to have to go in and do this manually for every single page. But the good news is that the end result will give your site a professional touch, which is well worth the effort.

Next, we're going to show you how to use these newfound skills to add the most important elements of your page - the 'keyword' and 'description' META Tags.

63

Inserting META Tags

'META Tags' are invisible commands stored within the HTML of a page that contain information about the document. You will have noticed with 'Word' in particular that there are already some META Tags in place showing that it was made using 'Word', when it was last edited and so on.

The two META Tags you are now going to add will contain useful data to let search engines (and those using them) know what the page is about - very much like the old fashioned index cards you used to see at the library.

If you want people to be able to find your page via search engines, you will first have to insert these tags into your HTML header.

The two extra META Tags you will need for your page are:
- A selection of KEYWORDS - this allows the search engine to decide how relevant your site is when a 'keyword' query is made.
- A short DESCRIPTION of the contents within the site - this appears as part of the search results offered for each query and helps the searcher to choose the best page from the results listed.

KEYWORDS - The code required is:
<META NAME=" KEYWORDS " CONTENT="keywords, here, separated, by, commas, and, a, space, unless, a, group, like, southern hemisphere, for, example">

Put some thought into your keywords and include as many different synonyms and related words on your subject as you can think of. You are allowed around 30 keywords per page, but if you run short it also pays to include a few misspellings of the most important keywords, as people using search engines generally make a *lot* of spelling mistakes.

Some Keyword Tips

- If it is important that any *sets* of words are seen as a group, then you should *not* separate them by commas (see 'southern hemisphere' in the example above).

- It's a good idea to make words plural wherever possible (or include the single *and* plural versions of a word if it spelled differently, rather than just having an 's' on the end).
- Include a word or two about the region you are located in, (country, state etc.). Even if your pages are meant to apply to web users world wide, people still search for local sites out of pure habit so it pays to include this information.

DESCRIPTION - The code required is:
<META NAME="DESCRIPTION" CONTENT="Useful information about so and so, particularly informative for those researching such and such.">

You are allowed about 1,000 characters for your description, but not all these will be displayed, so try to include the most important descriptive information first.

Before You Start

You'll remember that part of your research was searching for pages like yours and seeing what came up first. You may wish to do this again to refresh your memory. Take a close look at the pages that achieved top results, paying particular attention to the keywords that appear in the HTML header (there are instructions on how to view these in Chapter 2).

It will also pay you to do similar searches in different search engines. The top results should be more or less the same, but you will note that some search engines present the entire description, while others may only present the first few words or so. This will help to best gauge which information to include *first* in your 'description' and how brief you should make it.

Some would argue that you should only have to enter these META Tags into any pages you wish to submit to search engines. Usually, this means the main page and any generative pages you have made (you need to dangle your bait in the water if you want to get a bite or two). However, it should be noted that many search engines 'spider' sites that are submitted. 'Spidering' involves the search engine hunting beyond the main page and also indexing any connected pages. For this reason, it pays to add these META

The Net-Works Guide to...

Tags to *all* of your pages (with differing 'keywords' and 'descriptions' as required).

This extra measure would make a lot of sense to a company with a variety of products, in that those looking for *one* particular product may not know anything about the *type* of company that would sell it. In such a case, having a listing floating around the search engines regarding this specific product would get you a visitor that you otherwise would have missed out on.

Drafting and Inserting your META Tags

Even though you have put some thought into what your tags will say, it's probably best to draft these in a word processing document first, so you can chop and change them without fear of messing with your code.

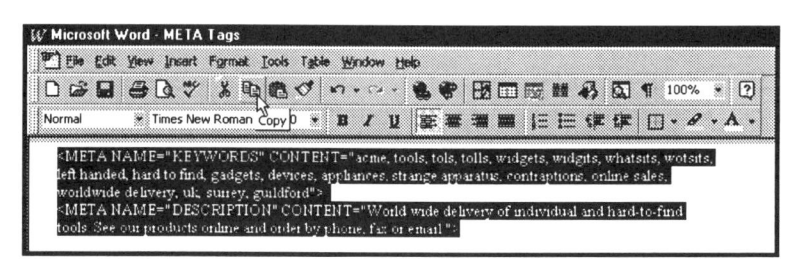

Note - when you save the word processing document, make sure you put it somewhere handy, but DO NOT save it to your special web site folder.

Once your META Tags are complete, highlight and 'Copy' the set of tags you wish to enter into a particular document.

Open the relevant HTML document in Word, then select the 'View' pull-down menu and click 'HTML Source'.

Place the cursor just in front of the </HEAD> part of the code, click

66

...Creating a Website

the 'Paste' button as shown, then press the 'Return' key on your keyboard.

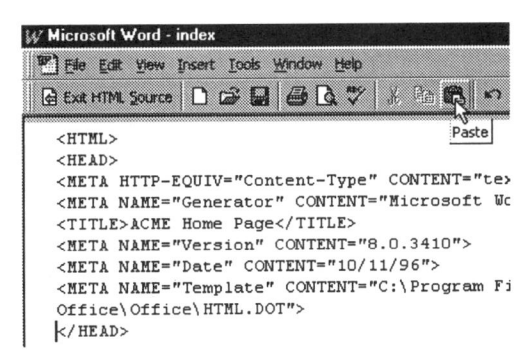

```
<HTML>
<HEAD>
<META HTTP-EQUIV="Content-Type" CONTENT="te>
<META NAME="Generator" CONTENT="Microsoft Wc
<TITLE>ACME Home Page</TITLE>
<META NAME="Version" CONTENT="8.0.3410">
<META NAME="Date" CONTENT="10/11/96">
<META NAME="Template" CONTENT="C:\Program Fj
Office\Office\HTML.DOT">
</HEAD>
```

You will see that your META Tags have been inserted into the 'head' of the HTML 'code'. Save your document, then click 'Exit HTML Source'.

Once all of your META Tags are in place and you are ready to upload your site and announce yourself to the world.

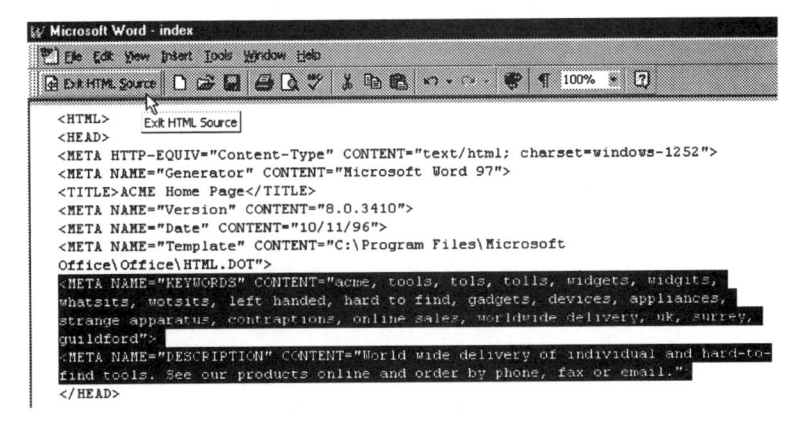

```
<HTML>
<HEAD>
<META HTTP-EQUIV="Content-Type" CONTENT="text/html; charset=windows-1252">
<META NAME="Generator" CONTENT="Microsoft Word 97">
<TITLE>ACME Home Page</TITLE>
<META NAME="Version" CONTENT="8.0.3410">
<META NAME="Date" CONTENT="10/11/96">
<META NAME="Template" CONTENT="C:\Program Files\Microsoft
Office\Office\HTML.DOT">
<META NAME="KEYWORDS" CONTENT="acme, tools, tols, tolls, widgets, widgits,
whatsits, wotsits, left handed, hard to find, gadgets, devices, appliances,
strange apparatus, contraptions, online sales, worldwide delivery, uk, surrey,
guildford">
<META NAME="DESCRIPTION" CONTENT="World wide delivery of individual and hard-to-
find tools. See our products online and order by phone, fax or email.">
</HEAD>
```

The Net-Works Guide to...

Chapter 12

Going Live

To upload your web site to it's web space, you will need an FTP (File Transfer Protocol) program. There are many different kinds of FTP programs available on the web (links to which will be available at the support site for this book). One of the most popular of these is the free program WS_FTP, which will be used as the example in this chapter.

Once you have downloaded and installed WS_FTP, you will need to configure it to make the process of uploading your pages as quick and easy as possible.

First, right-click on the icon that appears on the desktop after installation, and select 'Properties'.

You'll see in the highlighted window that WS_FTP is set to start in it's own folder. This means that every time you open the program, you will have to go hunting around for your special web site folder. To make your life much easier, just change the 'Start in' directory to the desired directory as shown. The location or name of your web site folder may be slightly different to that shown, but the principal is straightforward.

...Creating a Website

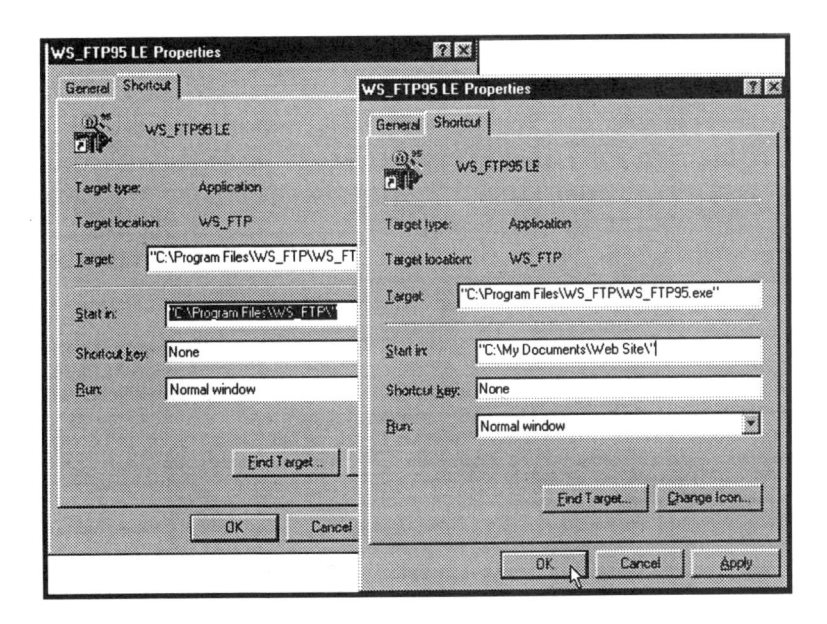

To open WS_FTP, you'll just have to double-click on the desktop icon.

The first time you use WS_FTP, you will have to tell it *where* to publish your web page files, and also give it the *authorisation information* your server requires. (These security precautions use your account User ID and password to ensure that only you can alter the contents of your web space.)

Click 'New', un-tick the 'Anonymous' box and tick the 'Save Password' box as shown, then enter the following information in the fields provided:

- **Profile Name**: 'My Web Page', 'Main Web Site' or something similar.
- **Host Name/Address**: This differs from server to server, but if you have a domain name, often it is as simple as entering your URL. In most cases, a quick email to your ISP or designated web server will get you these details.
- **User ID**: Here you will have to enter your user name. If your web space is hosted by your ISP, this is usually the text that

appears before the '@' on your MAIN email address, but some ISP's (just to be difficult) insist on the *entire* email address here.
- **Password:** Here you will have to enter your account password (if your web site is being hosted by your ISP, this is the same as your normal connection password).

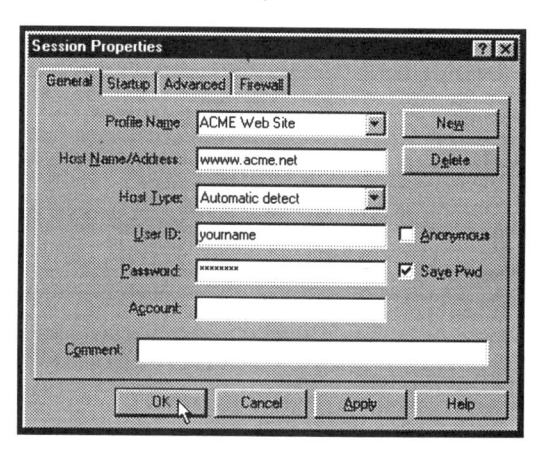

Now click 'Apply' to complete the new profile. WS_FTP is now configured to publish your web page files. To close WS_FTP, click 'Cancel', then 'Exit' WS_FTP. Or, if you wish, from here you can immediately connect to the Internet to upload your files to your web space. To do this click 'OK'.

Your computer will prompt you to connect to the Internet. If you have more than one connection, you will have to make sure that you are connecting to the right server with your Dial-up Connection (obviously you cannot upload to your web space folder if you are connecting to a different service provider - the folder just won't be there).

Once you connect successfully, you will not only be able to see all of the files relating to your newly constructed web site in the left-hand window, but also those at your web space on the right. (The first time you connect, of course, this folder will be empty, except in many cases for a single 'index' page put there by your ISP or server to announce that the web space has been reserved

...Creating a Website

for one of their users. In a few moments, your own index page will replace this one, giving visitors to your web space access to all of the pages you are about to upload.)

To transfer your files to this web space, simply click on each file you wish to add, then click the 'arrow' button that points to the right. In this instance, we can see that the templates created earlier are still in the special web site folder. Ideally, these should be relocated to another folder, but you can keep them here if you wish - just remember *not* to upload them!

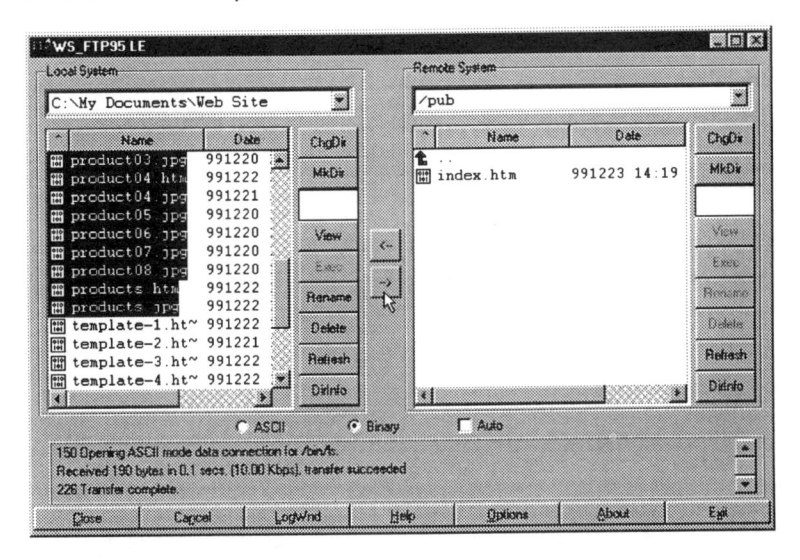

This window will appear briefly to show you the progress of each file's 'upload' to your web space folder - some will be quicker than others.

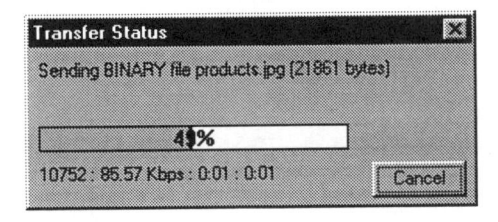

The Net-Works Guide to...

> **Hint - If you have only changed the text or links on a web page, you will not have to re-send the pictures or graphics for that page. However, if the changes you have made involve your pictures, then you will have to upload these amended graphics to your web space folder.**

When the transfer is complete, WS_FTP will show the uploaded files that have been copied to your web space in the right-hand window. Once you are done, click 'Exit' to close WS_FTP.

Updating Files

If you make any changes to your web pages, all you have to do is open WS_FTP and connect, highlight any files that are involved in the changes, then click the 'arrow' button that points to the right, to update the files. If there is a file on your web space with the same name as the one you are transferring, it will be replaced by the new version.

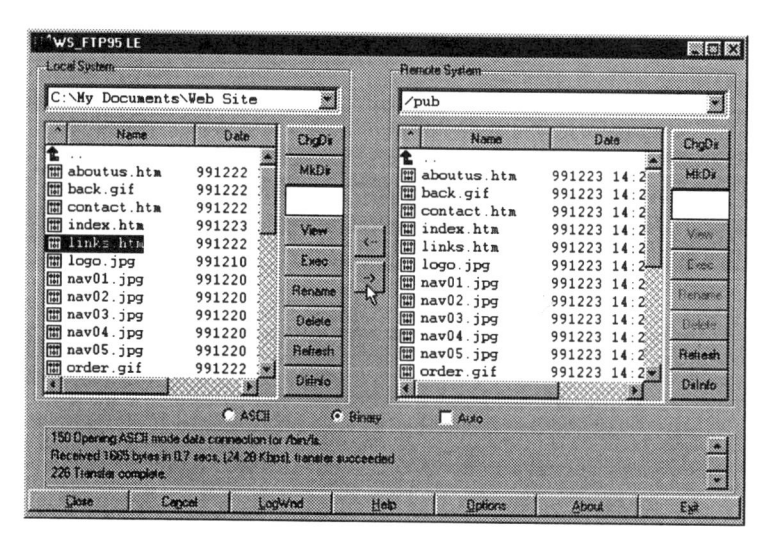

...Creating a Website

Hint - You will be able to choose multiple files by clicking on each one with your mouse as you hold down the 'Ctrl' button on your keyboard.

Deleting Files

If you wish to delete files from your web space, open WS_FTP and connect as usual, highlight any files you wish to delete, then click 'Delete' as shown.

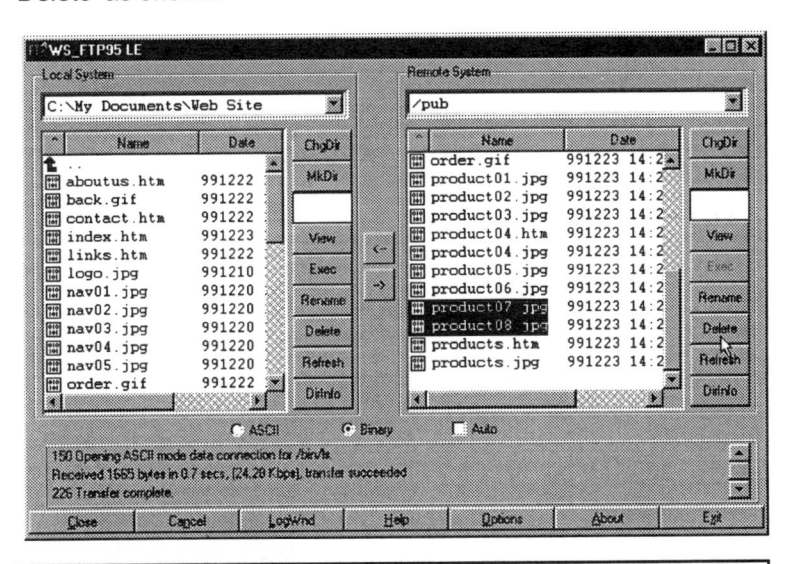

Note - You will note a 'stray' file has been saved to the special web site folder on your computer. This is the WS_FTP log, which keeps a record of the latest transfers for your reference. If you wish to view this file, simply highlight it in WS_FTP and click 'View'.

73

The Net-Works Guide to...

Viewing Your 'Live' Web Site

Your web site should be available to view online almost immediately.

Open your browser and connect to the Internet as usual. In the 'Address' window type your URL then press the 'Enter' key on your keyboard (if you do not have a domain name, or are unsure of your exact URL, then you will need to contact your ISP or server for this address).

Once your site is 'live', you should go through and check it again, paying particular attention to any graphics that may have failed to upload properly.

Though the site is now 'live', it is unlikely anybody will see it unless they know the exact URL. You may wish to forward this URL to a few trusted people to get them to check over the live version for a final 'test'. Once you are confident with your new site, it is time to get it listed with a few search engines so other web users can find it.

Chapter 13

Submitting to Search Engines

If you've been on the web for a while, you may have received a few items of Spam offering software or services that will "submit your site to thousands of search engines and directories at one low price". You should file these very carefully under 'D' for 'Delete', as they are a waste of time and money.

For the most part, you will only need to submit your site to a dozen or so of the larger search engines - and perhaps a few of the specialised or local directories you found while doing your research.

To begin with, it's probably best just to register with one or two engines manually. To do this, go to each search engine in turn and look for a link on their main page saying 'Add URL' or 'Submit URL'. Follow this link to the submission form and submit your page.

Different engines require different levels of information, but for the most part all they will ask for is the URL (individual web address) of the page and your email address (so they can confirm the entry of your page into their database and/or alert you of any problems).

> **Hint** - The easiest way to make sure the URL you are submitting is correct is to view your web page online and 'Copy' the entire text that appears in the 'Address' window of your browser. You can then 'Paste' this text into the submission form at the search engine(s) of your choice.

Submitting a web page to a search engine is, mostly, free. If you do encounter any search engines or directories that require you to pay in order to list your page, then ask yourself carefully if the expense is worth it. Usually, it isn't. The only time you should consider parting with money for a listing in a search engine or directory is if it is a large and well-publicised one (such as an online version of your local yellow pages).

It will take a few days (and sometimes a few weeks) for your page(s) to be included in the search engine database, so be patient. The easiest way to check if you are listed is to type your entire URL in the 'Search' box and click 'Search'. If you're in there, it will find you.

Once your entry appears, you will see how useful your 'description' META Tag is to people looking for your page. It is these few words that often mean the difference between people choosing your site over another search engine result.

The reason we have advised you to only submit to one or two engines at first is because you may feel you need to make a few changes to your 'description' and/or 'keywords' once you have viewed them in action. If you do make any changes to your META Tags, you will then have to upload the new version of the page to your web server, then re-submit the related page to the search engines so the latest version of the 'description' will appear in the search results.

Note - You won't have to re-submit your page each time you change it, only when you alter the META Tags.

You may also want to play around with your keywords a bit after a few experiments. To find out how useful (or suitable) your keywords are, try typing a few of the words you have used and see what kind of 'ranking' you get for different combinations of these words - in other words, how high up the search results you appear; is it first, fifth of fiftieth?

Once you have settled on a good description and some powerful keywords, then you can submit your new page far and wide with confidence.

Multiple Submissions

There are a number of sites - and even some software - that will let you submit your page(s) to many of the majorsearch engines quickly and easily (there will be some links to some services that are free or represent excellent value at the support web page for this book).

Web Sites

These vary in the level of service they provide, and what they ask for in return. Often they will ask you to put a link to their site on your web page.

Alternatively, they may send email to the address you have used for the submission to promote their 'paid for' services. As incredible as it may seem, some even offer the service without asking for a thing, as they use the submission facility to drive people to their site (yes, this is an example of a 'generative' page).

If you feel guilty about getting something for nothing in this way, you can return the favour simply by having a poke around the site and visiting a few of the featured products or sponsors.

You should look elsewhere if they start asking you for money, as there are plenty of free services about.

Software

There is even some software available that will let you enter your page details, then submit them to multiple search engines at the click of a button. Full versions of this kind of software nearly always cost money, but there are often free 'trial' versions available that work for a limited time and/or limit submissions to the top ten directories (and this is all most of us really need).

Getting Better Results

Even if someone using a search engine enters two or three of the keywords you have included in your site, there may be thousands of others with equally relevant keywords. Search engines have different methods of judging in which order they are going to place a set of sites with equal keyword relevance, and ideally you want to be one of the top ten results. There are a number of ways to achieve this, simply by being more aware of how these different systems work.

One way search engines decide on ranking is by gauging the number of 'hits' the site has received through them in the past. You will notice here that we used the word 'site' and not 'page'. This is because the 'hit count' in such instances is often gauged by total visits to *all* of your pages, not just the one involved in any given search. So you can see how your 'generative' page(s) need not relate directly to the products or services within your site to be of use to you. Even though thousands of web users visiting these unrelated pages may have no interest in what else you have on offer, their very presence at your site will help improve the ranking of the pages that really *do* count.

Other search engines may judge the importance of a page or site by the number of other sites listed with them that that link to it. Here you can see why so many sites request a link in exchange for a 'free' service, and why it pays to get others to link to your site (no matter how relevant their site is to yours). Of course, to do you any good, the site that links to you will have to be listed with the search engine in question, but you could very well offer to do this in exchange for the link.

As you can see, good search engine results take a lot of time and planning. This said, not many web users know how to list their pages properly, so with this information (and a few tricks such as misspelled 'keywords') you should see some quite promising results within four to eight weeks.

How Not to Promote Your Web Site

After all of your hard work, you may feel frustrated by a lack of immediate results. Don't be.

For a start, it may take some time for you to fine-tune your site and get all of the bugs out. This makes the delay in getting 'listed' an effective 'cooling off' period that you should take advantage of. Secondly, most of the methods used to immediately announce a web site are more than likely to get you into trouble.

Newsgroups

The first thing most people do when they get a new web site up and running is to dive into a few newsgroups and post a message saying announcing its launch. This is known as 'Usenet Spam' and you definitely shouldn't do it - especially if you are not a regular member of the newsgroup you are posting to. Most replies to such a message will be along the lines of 'get lost', 'I went to your page and it was crap', or even worse, 'I object to this off-topic Spam and have sent a complaint to your ISP'. If you feel you must promote your site through a newsgroup, then make sure it is relevant in topic and *participate* in the group. If you do this, no one will object to you having a link to your site within your 'signature'.

Email

Unsolicited email, otherwise known as 'Spam', is the lowest common denominator of online promotion and should be avoided at all costs. Again, you can include a link to your site in your signature when replying to an email, but sending out new mail plugging your site to all and sundry will not make you any friends.

Chat Rooms

Promoting web sites within chat rooms is widely forbidden, and is more likely to get you automatically kicked out than get visitors to your site.

Chapter 14

The Future - Adding a few extras

As you grow in confidence, you may wish to add a few extras to your site to make it more functional. Again, we are going to warn you *not* to get carried away. You shouldn't add something to your site just because you've learned a new trick and want to show off.

Enquiry and Feedback Forms

An online form is very easy to make, (Microsoft Word provides a function to help you make forms quickly and easily) but these forms rely heavily on the CGI capacity of your web space - and different servers have different ways of accepting and organising this information.

For this reason, you will need to contact your ISP or server for information regarding the making of online forms. Often, if the process is a difficult one, packaged solutions are provided that you can customise for your site.

If the space your site is to be hosted or does not have CGI capability, then there are several tools and gadgets on the web that will let you include a form in your site without any of these problems. The downside to this is that the page your form appears on will no doubt include advertising that you have little or no control over.

For this reason it pays to choose carefully, but there will be links to the best of such services on the support web page for this book.

Web Counters and Trackers
Counters are very useful in that they provide information about the popularity of your site. You can then use this data to gauge how successful your efforts have been (and make plans on how to improve the results).

Servers that have the necessary CGI capability for this will often provide users with a code that they can easily enter into their HTML, to activate a counter specific to their account. Unfortunately, this is usually only available for one page of your site and simply counts the number of visitors to that page, so if you want more information you will have to look further afield.

There is a wide range of tracking software available, but again this counts a lot on the individual CGI capabilities of your server. Often it pays to investigate a 'virtual' or 'proxy' package as this can work via any server and takes a lot of the hassle and expense out of your tracking needs.

There are a wide variety of such counters and trackers available through the web, many of which are free. They vary in function from the most basic counters, to full tracking capabilities that can let you know things like how visitors to your site found you and how long they stayed. Links to the best of such services will also be available at our support web page.

Maps
If yours is a business site and you wish to include a map of your location, then you may be happy to know that there is a quick and simple solution. Many of the online map services available are not only free to use, but are more than happy for you to link to them. Some even let you include a link on your site to a map complete with a circle or other highlight showing your exact location. Again, functions and conditions of service differ, but you'll find links to the best of such services at the support web page for this book.

New Content
Depending on how popular your site is, you may wish to update the content or add new material as time allows. This not only encourages users to return to your site regularly, but also helps your

web site to grow in size. For instance, if you write one article a month and publish it on your main page, it doesn't make any sense to throw the old articles away - especially when you can 'archive' this past material and make it available to your visitors, thereby adding value and depth to your site.

A New Design

As the content of your pages should occasionally change, so too should the 'look' and 'feel' of the site. Every now and then it is a good idea to give your site a complete overhaul, changing anything from the way it looks to the way it functions. You may have to do this sooner rather than later on your very first effort, but once you 'get it right', you should still cast an appraising eye over it once every six to twelve months.

The clever way to do this is to keep a note of any problems the current site may be experiencing (and any ideas you may have along the way). You can then use these notes to recreate your site in the best way possible.

A Final Word

One thing you should definitely *not* add to your site is an 'under construction' sign. This makes it look as if you are apologising for the state of your site, and has the same effect as introducing a joke with "It's kind of weak, are you sure you want me to tell it?" It's also highly unnecessary, as nearly every other site on the web is constantly evolving. Just as yours should be...

...Creating a Website

Chapter 15

Some Helpful Web Sites

Remember to visit this book's webpage at www.networks.co.uk/create.htm for updates to this section. You'll find links to all of the sites mentioned here, and they'll be updated for any changes in URL.

Adding Gadgets to Your Site

As we mentioned earlier, if you have limited coding knowledge or a lack of CGI facilities at your server, you may need a little outside help to add some more involved tools to your site.

Microsoft bCentral
http://www.bcentral.com/

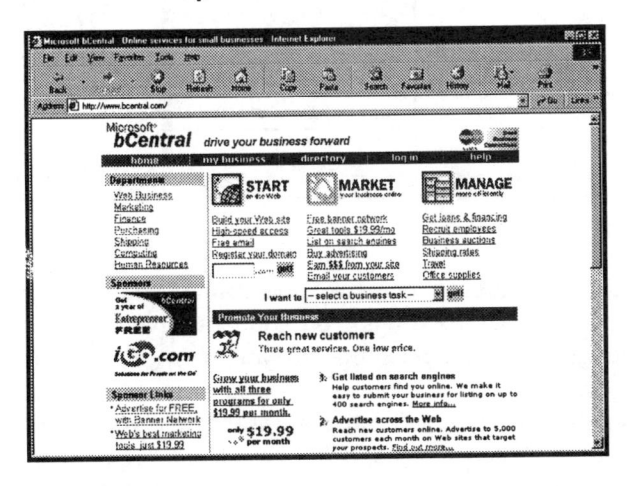

This is primarily a business portal for Microsoft, so they do spend a lot of time trying to sell you their products - and tend to bury the free stuff where you can't find it! However, with a bit of patience and perseverance you can find some very useful tools here, including one of the best 'proxy' web counters on the web - FastCounter. (Because this is so hard to find on the Microsoft site, we've put a direct link to it on our support web page.)

Also available here are some of the largest free banner and link exchange programs on the web. But remember that biggest does not always mean best...

MyComputer.com
http://www.mycomputer.com/

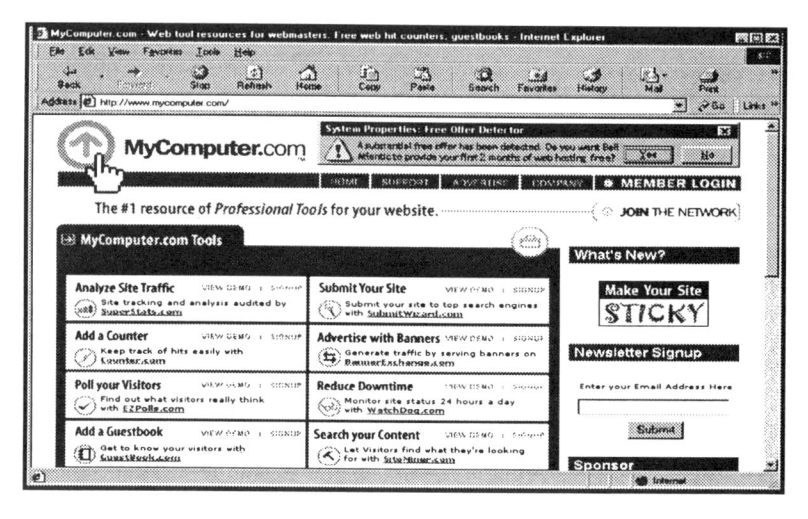

By far the best source for 'proxy' tools and gadgets to enhance your site. Not only will you find great counters and trackers here, but also guestbooks and polls (so you can get feedback from your visitors).

Again, they will try to sell you a few products along the way. But, in contrast to Microsoft's site, all the free stuff is easy to find. The free tools available are not only well designed and packed with features, but easy to customise and add to your site.

Attracting and Tracking Visitors to Your Site

If you really want more visitors to your site, you need to be up on the latest search engine developments. There are also a few tips and shortcuts you may wish to take advantage of, and the following sites will be more than useful here.

Search Engine Watch
http://www.searchenginewatch.com/

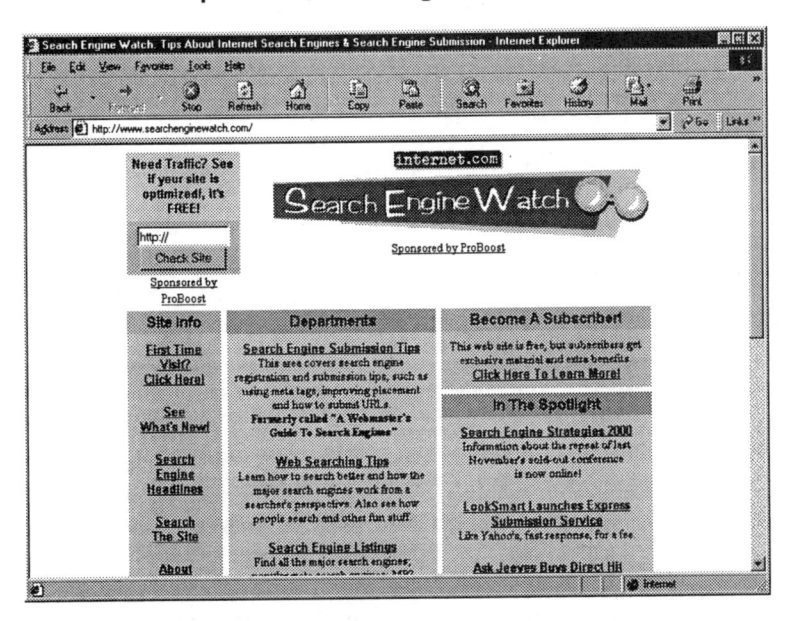

This site is devoted to search engines and how they work. If you're serious about using them to their best effect, then a visit to this site is a must. There are regular news items about recent developments, new search engines and more. Also featured are tutorials on how to best use search engines to find what you want - and improve the placement of your own site.

Open Directory Project
http://dmoz.org/

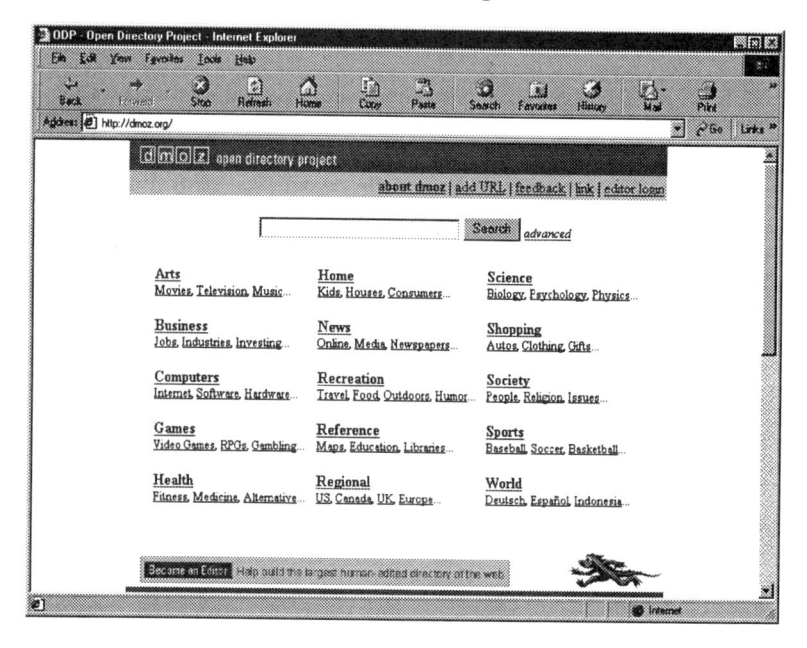

If you do plan on submitting your site to a few search engines, then this should be your first port of call. It's very easy to do, you just find a category that you think your web site belongs in and submit your URL. In this way, the Open Directory Project works just like Yahoo, with one very big difference - people just like you are the editors, and there are thousands upon thousands of them.

The best thing about this situation is that the OPD has so many editors that your listing can appear within 24 hours in some cases - meaning immediate results (a rare thing with search engines).

Even better, the Open Directory Project is now being used by Lycos, HotBot and many other major search engines to beef up their own 'category' sections. Every few weeks these larger engines scan through and add new entries directly from the OPD, and when this happens you will find that your single entry at the OPD has you listed across the web with a number of other major 'category' databases. Also, each category listing you have counts as a link to your page within other search engines - increasing your result ranking here also.

Search Engine Garage
http://www.searchenginegarage.com/

There are many sites available on the web that will let you submit to a number of search engines at once. Many of these are 'free', but they aren't always easy to use and there's nearly always a catch (like requiring that you put a banner or link on your site).

The Search Engine Garage is refreshingly different in that it will allow you to submit your site to the top 30 search engines with no strings attached. And, while it may not look simple, you will find it far easier to use than any other service on offer. Once you have made your first submission the site automatically fills in the details you need for additional search engines, so for the most part you just have to press 'Go' for each one in turn. As you do this, it then lets you see the confirmation of each submission in the main window, making it much more informative and reliable than some of the 'set and forget' services on offer.

The Net-Works Guide to...

spyonit.com
http://www.spyonit.com/

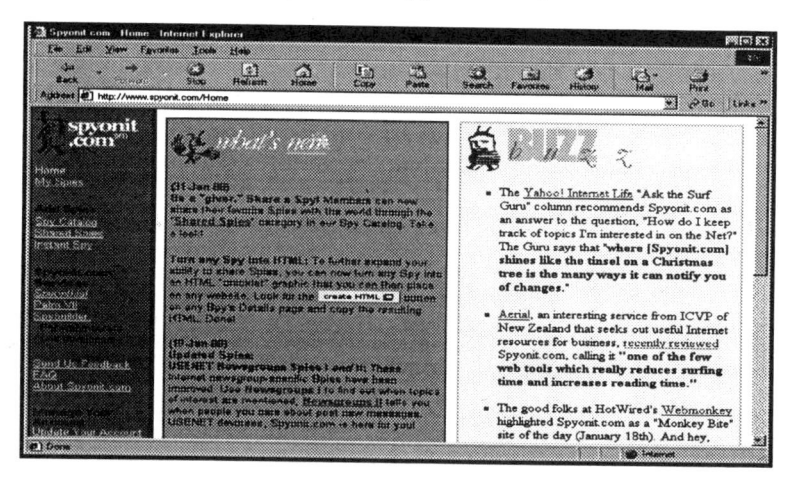

'Spyonit' is a powerful and almost omnipresent tool that constantly scans the web for the latest information. On offer is a choice of 'Spies' that you can configure to tell you when something on the web has changed in a certain way. A lot of people use this to find out when there is a new recipe at Gourmet.com, or when 'Sound of Music' is going to be on television in their area, but the craftier web users make good use of the 'Swiss Army Spies'.

Just to give you an example or two, you can set a 'Swiss Army Spy' to let you know when someone mentions or links to you, or when one of your competitors goes online with their own web site. You can even set it to monitor newsgroups and notify you when your name is mentioned. Those building a commercial presence on the web would do well to use this powerful information tool.

Checking Your Site
Even though your site may look right, there may be a few minor technical glitches here and there that stop some users from seeing it properly or enjoying it fully. The following sites will help you fix these problems.

Web Site Garage
http://www.websitegarage.com/

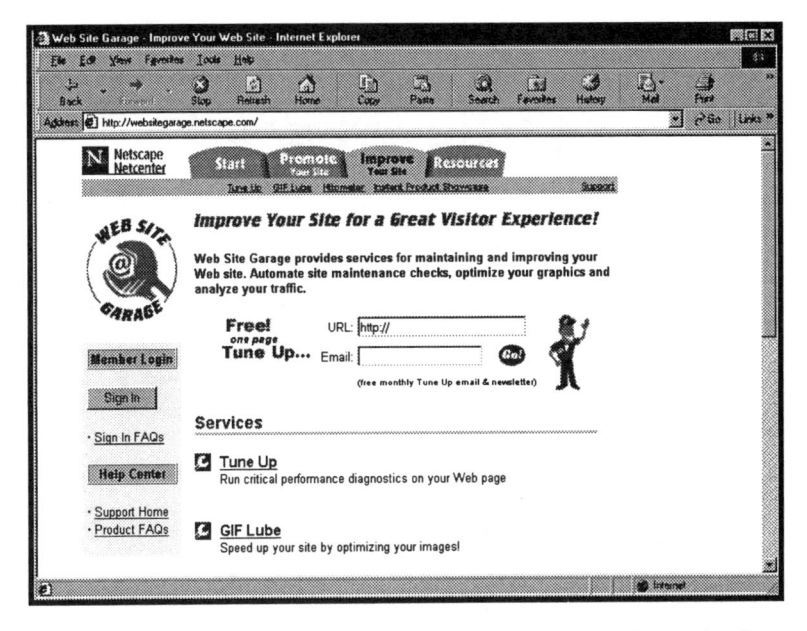

The first thing you want to hit the Web Site Garage for is the free 'five point web site tune-up'. In just a few moments this handy tool provides you with a concise review of how well your page functions, from the basic code, to how fast it loads - plus how ready it is for submission to search engines.

Of course, along the way, the nice folks from Web Site Garage are going to try to sell you a few of their products or services, but the site provides plenty of free resources and information that should be more than adequate for the home user. Check out the Resources section in particular for regular articles on the art of building a beautiful, and functional, web page (there is also a related mailing list available here).

Doctor HTML
http://www2.imagiware.com/RxHTML/

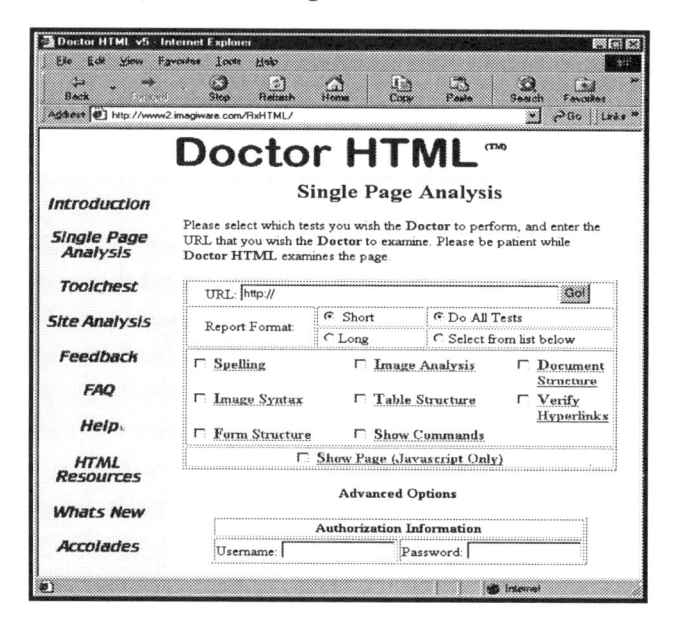

Doctor HTML works very much like the Web Site Garage, but takes a much closer look at the code and structure of any individual page you care to have it examine. It will let you know if there are any problems with your tables or forms - and will even cast a questioning eye over your spelling!

Bobby
http://www.cast.org/bobby/

Bobby is a completely free service intended to make sure that web pages remain informative for the entire community - including the disabled. To this end, they will check your page for free to make sure it is accessible by those with vision problems or any other disabilities that require them to use special software to access web sites.

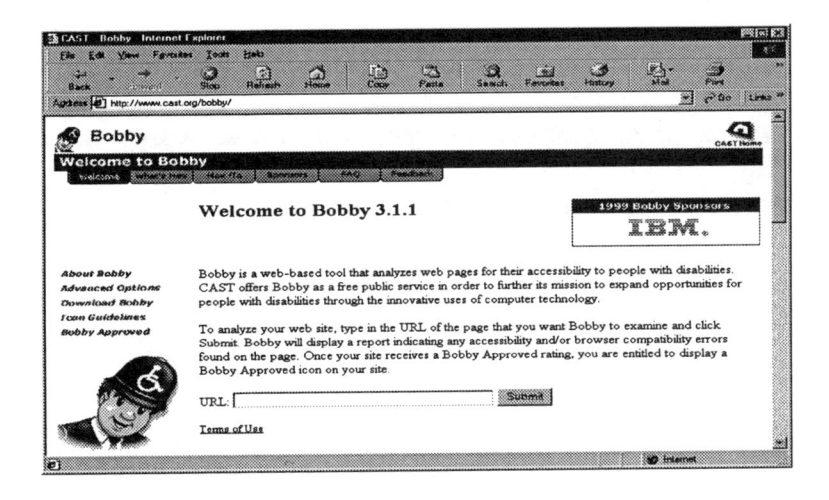

You may not think this necessary, but many of the things Bobby checks are essential to good design. Some of the things it will report on include basic browser compatibility, how straightforward and descriptive your headers and links are, and whether there is alternative text for any images you may have on your page. This is important not only to the vision impaired, but also to the many web users who have their browser set to ignore graphics.

Downloads and Other Freebies

You may wish to try a new authoring program, or check out some of the free graphics and animation software available in your quest for a better web site. Well, one of the great things about the web is the huge amount of software available, and how much of it is free.

Download.com
http://download.cnet.com/

One of the best spin-offs of Cnet's huge site is this very handy and easy to use download centre. Here you can browse through thousands of downloadable programs either by type or operating platform (like Mac or PC), or use the comprehensive search function to find a specific program.

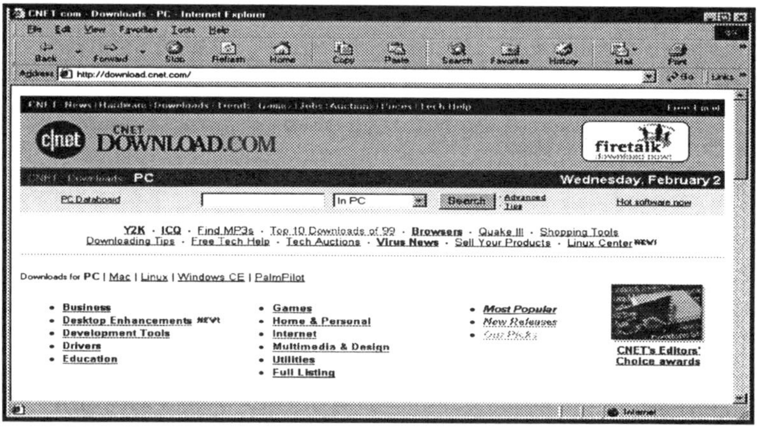

The programs available are too numerous and varied to mention - but if it's free, fun or functional you can bet it's available here. Most programs are free or shareware, download sizes are clearly labelled and most come with their own review. Of course, should the file be a large one it will take a while to download - but this doesn't stop you from browsing other sites while you wait.

Tudogs

http://www.tudogs.com/

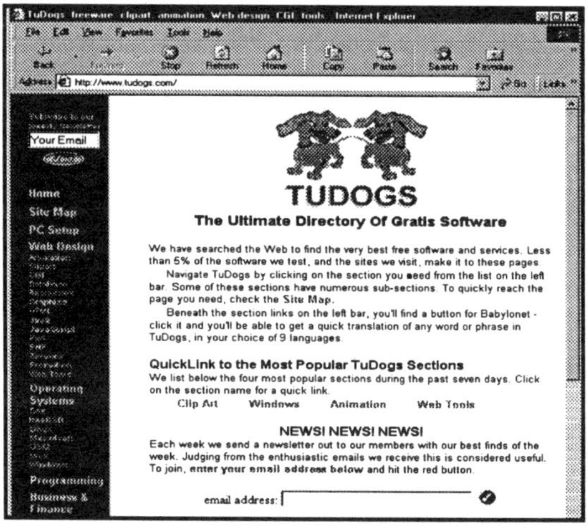

Tudogs also has many downloadable programs available, but specialises in those that are free. It also features links to some of the best graphics and animations on the web, also available absolutely free (for use on personal web pages). This is a very useful site that will save you a lot of fruitless searching.

Beyond Basic Authoring

If you find you have a flair for making web pages and are feeling somewhat restricted by the limitations of an authoring package like Word, then it's time to take the next step into HTML - and beyond.

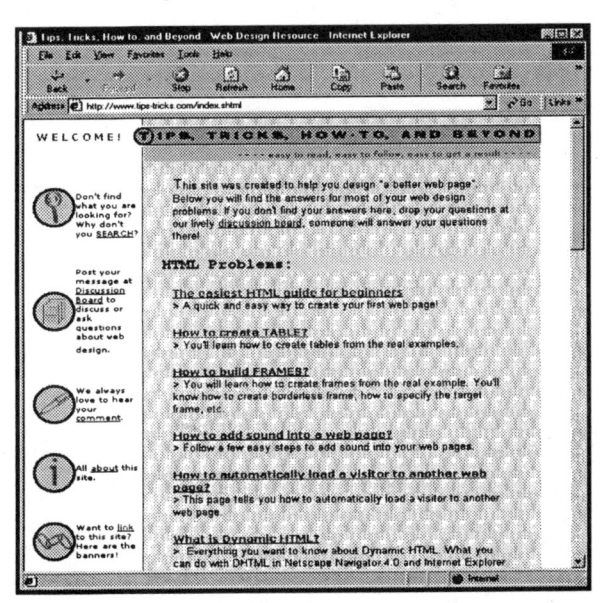

Tips, Tricks, How to and Beyond
http://www.tips-tricks.com/

This is not only a great place to start if you want to learn HTML from scratch, but also covers a lot of extra information beyond simple code. Should you not find what you are looking for here, there is also a discussion board so you can ask questions.

A Beginner's Guide to HTML
http://www.ncsa.uiuc.edu/General/Internet/WWW/

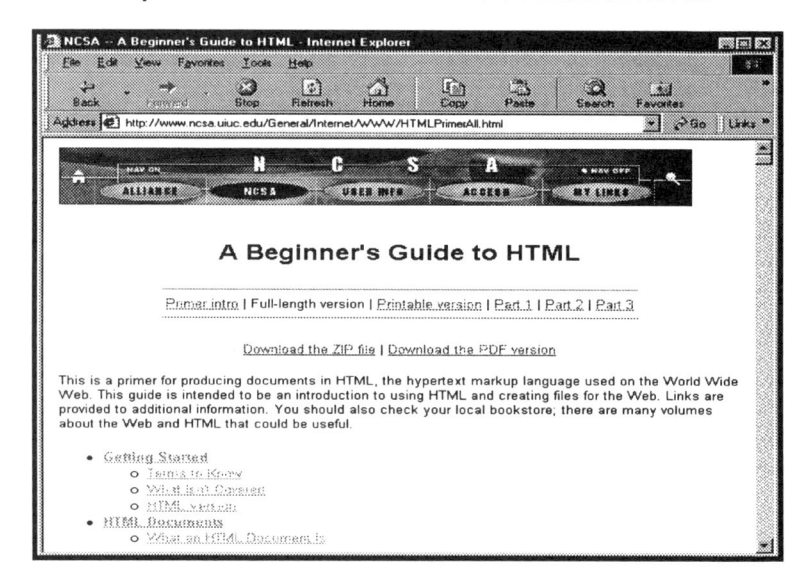

An excellent and very popular introduction to the basics of HTML from the folks at the National Computational Science Alliance (US). While this guide won't teach you everything about HTML, it's very straightforward and easy to print so you can pore over it with a cup of coffee (or two).

Professional Web Design and HTML Tutorials
http://junior.apk.net/~jbarta/

This is more of a step-by-step affair than the previous two sites, and is much friendlier in tone. ("Hello. My name is Joe and I'm going to give you a few simple lessons on how to make frames for your web documents.")

You will not only find the tutorials here very easy to follow, but also useful in terms of achieving a single effect that your usual authoring program does not cater for. It is then a very simple matter to insert the new feature into your code and carry on as normal.

...Creating a Website

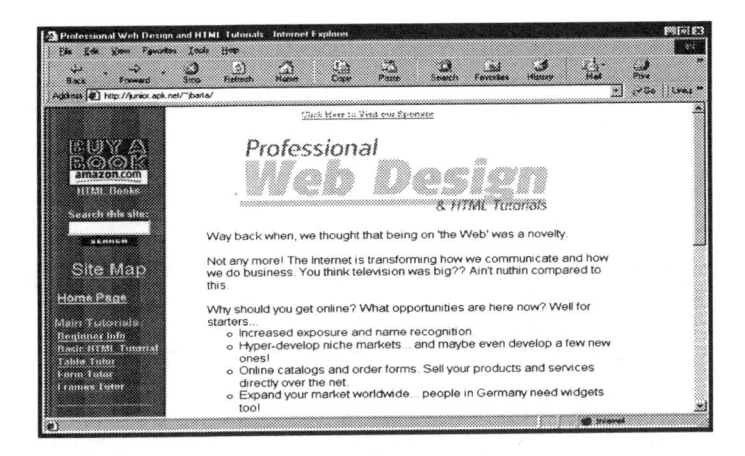

HTML Goodies
http://www.htmlgoodies.com/

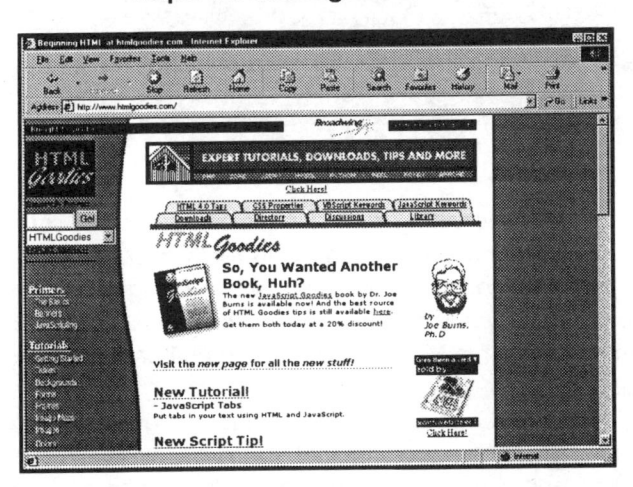

Again, this is a great site for little tips and tricks to help you improve on the limited results authoring programs can achieve. There will be many shortcuts and code tricks available here that will help you make your web page much more functional without having to learn any more HTML than you need to know.

The Net-Works Guide to...

The site even has some more advanced tools such as Javascript available, but for more on this you may also wish to visit the equally excellent 'JavaScript World' at www.jsworld.com.

Webmonkey
http://www.webmonkey.com/

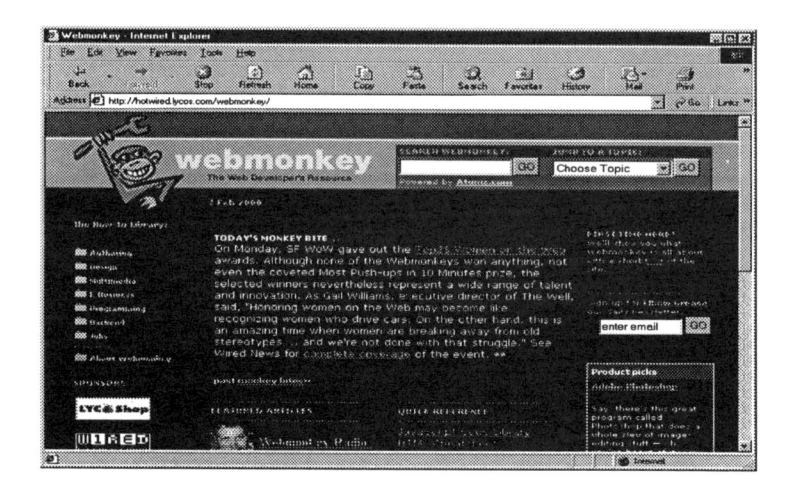

We've covered everything from learning basic HTML to some more advanced features, but for those who really wish to get into web authoring, Webmonkey does it all. While being one of the best resources for advanced programmers the world over, it still finds time to include some HTML basics and even has a special section for kids.

While the quirky writing style may not be to everyone's taste, there is certainly no arguing that Webmonkey is the very best education and community web site for those who are genuinely serious about authoring (and little else).

Glossary

Access provider
May also be referred to as an ISP (Internet Service Provider). A company which will sell you an Internet connection. It will have installed its own FTP, Gopher, Archie, news, mail and Web servers and will provide you with the necessary software to use them.

Anonymous FTP
A way of logging in to a computer and downloading files by FTP without having to identify yourself (so you don't need TCP/IP). Usually you log in as Anonymous and use your Email address as the password.

Backbone
High speed data connections which join together the big access providers. Smaller access providers need to connect to a backbone provider to gain access to the backbone. In WAN's it is the central section of the network.

Baud rate
Used mainly when referring to the speed of modems. It is the speed at which data can travel along a channel, in terms of bits per second.

Binary
Computers work by counting in ones or zeros which is known as binary. Files stored on a computer may be either binary or ASCII. In a binary file the data is stored in seven-bit bytes; in an ASCII file data is stored in eight-bit bytes. Most systems can read ASCII files but not all can read binary files. Programs are usually binary files, while Emails are more likely to be simple ASCII files. Most Email packages do not allow the transfer of binary files.

Bits/Bytes
A bit is the smallest piece of information that a computer recognises and it's either got a value of zero or one. A byte is a group of either seven-bits or eight-bits.

Bps
Bits per second. The speed at which data can be transferred between pieces of hardware. You are most likely to come across it in relation to how fast modems work.

Browser
To download and read documents taken from the World Wide Web you need a software program called a browser. The most common are from Netscape, Mosaic and Microsoft.

Client
Software on a computer which is used to request information from the Internet. When you call up a web page you are acting as the client, and the computer you have contacted is the 'server'.

Dialup
A non-permanent connection to the Internet. A dial-up account will not use TCP/IP, so whilst connected you can not be recognised by the rest of the Internet.

Domain name
An Internet identification name that specifies where your computer can be contacted. It is written as a series of letters separated by full stops and slashes; for instance ours is net-works.co.uk

Download
The process of copying a file from one machine (usually the host) to another (usually yours).

Email address
An address which identifies you on the Internet and allows others to send you Email. There may be many people at a domain name,

so the Email address can identify a particular person at a particular address. It is made up from your name, the symbol @ (pronounced at), and the domain name. e.g. sales@net-works.co.uk.

FAQ
Frequently Asked Questions. This is a document found in most Usenet groups. It will have questions (and answers) that are most commonly asked by newcomers to the group. Read it before you post any questions in a group.

Flame
A rude message usually posted to a group or individual. Flames are considered offensive and those who do it will find themselves shunned. A flame often incites retaliation with horrible consequences. Do not get involved in flame throwing.

Firewall
It will not protect you from flames, but it is a security measure. It prevents access to a LAN from outside networks, e.g. from the Internet. Many companies do not want others to be able to access their LAN.

Gateway
A device which translates an incoming flow of data from an outside network so that it can be used on a LAN. A gateway can be shared by many users.

Gopher
Software that can search the Internet and find information for you. You need to have a Gopher client on your machine and the host machine must have a Gopher server application. Most web browsers now have a Gopher facility. Gopher is menu driven and it will read and download documents based on your selection criteria. These documents can then be read off-line.

Home page
It has two meanings. It is the first page of a company's web site

The Net-Works Guide to...

and the one you will be taken to as a default. It is also a generic term for the whole web site of a company or individual.

Host
Another computer on the Internet which allows users to connect to it. An ISP's computer is a host computer.

HTML
Hypertext mark-up language. You need to know this language to create documents to go on the World Wide Web.

HTTP
Hypertext Transfer Protocol. The way to transfer HTML documents between the client and the Web server (so others can then see them on the WWW).

Hypertext
Text on your computer screen which you click to take you to another document in the same web site or at another. Hypertext links form the basis of the World Wide Web. When creating a web site the author uses HTML to put up hypertext.

ISP
See Access Provider.

IP
Internet Protocol. This is a standard which devices on the Internet use to communicate with each other. It describes how data gets from its source to its destination.

IP address
Your Email address uniquely tells the Internet who you are. Computers need to know this but they prefer to deal in numbers so your Email address has a decimal notation known as your IP address.

IRC
Internet Relay Chat. An Internet resource allowing you to chat in real time to anyone else connected to the same chat room.

ISDN
Integrated Services Digital Network. It is a network which allows you to send information in a digital form over the existing telephone lines at speeds of 128Kb. You dial up the computer you wish to access, establish a connection and send your information very quickly. ISDN lines can be installed by BT but they are more expensive to install and rent than a normal telephone line.

LAN
Local area network. A group of computers and peripherals connected together to form a network where they can talk to each other. They can vary in size from just computers in an office to hundreds across several buildings.

Metasearch
A search engine that works by querying other search engines.

Modem
MOdulator DEModulator. A device which can send and receive information. It either receives information from your computer, converts it into analogue signals, and then passes them down the telephone line to another computer. Or, it takes a signal from a telephone line and converts it into a form your computer can understand. Modems operate at different speeds.

Moderator
A person who checks all the messages received by a newsgroup ensuring they are on topic. Cynics call them censors.

Newsgroup
Internet bulletin boards where you can find out everything there is to know. There are thousands for every subject imaginable and collectively they are known as Usenet.

Packet
Data that is bundled up before being sent across a network is called a packet. It has information such as where it has come from, where it is going, what is in it and what form it is in so that the recipient computer can read it.

POP
Point of Presence. An access point set up by an Access Provider. There will be many around the country so that you can make a local priced call to a POP and then get on to the Internet.

PPP
Point to Point Protocol. It allows IP connections between two devices over both types of circuits. When you connect to your ISP you are probably using a PPP connection.

Protocol
A standard for how two devices communicate with each other, like a common language.

Router
Connects together all the networks that make up the Internet and allows the transfer of packets.

Server
A central computer, often a dedicated PC, which makes data available to the Internet.

SLIP
Serial Line Internet Protocol. Now being superseded by PPP, it is a standard which allows devices to use IP over asynchronous and synchronous links.

Spam
Internet slang for when someone indiscriminately sends the same message to various newsgroups. No one appreciates it.

TCP
Transmission Control Protocol. The major standard of all the Internet Protocols. TCP makes sure packets get from one host to another and that what they contain is understood. It takes the data to be transmitted from the application and passes it onto the IP for transmission.

Unix
An operating system running on a host machine that allows many clients to access the host's information, at the same time. Used by many of the servers on the Internet.

Upload
When you send a file or message from a computer (usually yours) to another computer (usually the host) you have uploaded your data.

WAIS
Wide Area Information Server. Allows a client to do a keyword search on several online databases at the same time.

WWW
World Wide Web. Commonly known simply as 'The Web', it has opened up the Internet to mass world-wide use. All documents on the web are hypertext-based which means they can all be linked together. You pass from one to the next by clicking on a particular word. Could soon become the definition of The Internet.

Zip File
A compressed file with the extension *.zip – not to be confused with a Zip drive.

Appendix

A Very Short History of the Internet

Way back in the good old days of the cold war, some bright spark realised that once the bombs started to drop any central communications network would be less than likely to stay intact. This meant that their computers would not be able to exchange information, codes etc. - thus drastically reducing the opportunity to drop more bombs. What they created to combat this was a system that allowed their computers to connect to another via any remaining connections and transfer the information in 'packets'. In this way, the route the information took would be unimportant, as the information 'packets' could be reassembled at the other end regardless of how they got there.

Soon after, non-military organisations such as universities and research agencies got in on the act and started using the system to share information.

What really opened the system up, however, was the development of HTML (Hyper Text Mark-up Language). This allowed data from any source to be read by a number of different operating systems. The subsequent development of 'browsers' that could view such documents led to much wider use of this system of sharing information. In effect, anybody with a computer and connection could publish a text document on what was known as the World Wide Web.

By 1993, public use of this medium was increasing exponentially. The more people used it, the more it improved. The recent explosion in commercial interest has only served to open it up even more, to the point that getting online is now cheaper and easier than it has ever been.

Think of all of those wonderfully expensive television programmes that you get to watch absolutely free if you are willing to put up with a few ad breaks. It's the same principle at work, except in this case the medium allows you to produce a commercial of your own and make it available to millions for next to nothing.

Some Common Misconceptions

? *I have to stay connected to use email*
✔ You do not have to be online to read or write email, just to send or receive it. When someone sends you an email, it waits in a private box at your server until you connect to collect it - you then disconnect to read any mail you have received. You will not miss any emails because you are not connected when it is sent to you.

? *I have to stay connected for my web page to be live*
✔ You don't have to be connected to the Internet for your web pages to be 'live', as they are stored on your server and available to anyone who wishes to see them - 24 hours a day, seven days a week.

? *Someone viewing my web page has access to my computer*
✔ Only the information you have published to your web space is accessible to web users. There is no direct connection to your computer.

? *I need to learn HTML coding to build a web page*
✔ We're sure that there are many coders and programmers who would have you believe this. But in truth, there are many web authoring packages and tools that enable the average computer user to create a serious web presence from their desktop with only a passing knowledge of HTML.

? *150 million users = 150 million customers*
✔ It would not be true to say that you have access to 150 million users - in truth, it is the 150 million users who have access to you - and not all of them will be looking for, or interested in, what you have to sell. The trick is in targeting your potential customers and making sure that they find their way to your site.

? There are millions of web pages - no one will be able to find me!
✔ Nonsense. Again, it comes down to an understanding of how the web works. In fact, in this book we show you the quite simple measures you need to take to be found by those who are looking for your kind of business.

? Advertising is unwelcome on the Internet
✔ While it is true some of the more blatant methods of advertising are not tolerated in certain Internet communities, clever marketing is another matter entirely (this attitude is not particular to the web - think how popular unsolicited phone calls are). Soft sell is the order of the day, and if your page has content that represents value to the consumer, then all the better.

? You can make lots of money overnight on the Internet
✔ Oh, be reasonable. While the Internet does provide you with many new, exciting, (and often free) ways of promoting your business, it is not a magic cure-all. Like any business effort, it will require careful strategy, planning and lots of hard work.

? The Internet is a waste of time and is unlikely to make you any money at all
✔ This kind of reaction usually comes from those who have tried and failed - mostly because they have ignored or failed to grasp the individual marketing principles that apply to the Internet. For them, it's much easier to blame the Internet in general than accept the fact that they failed to understand the medium and/or implement a successful business plan.

What the Internet Will Mean to Your Business
With good planning and a solid foundation, your Internet presence should become part of your regular promotional and sales schedule. It will not magically replace your need to promote your business in more traditional forms or lead to a million sales in the very first week, but carefully nurtured it will grow into a regular - and possibly even primary - facet of your business.

Starting and Running a Business on the Internet

Do you want to:
- ✔ Sell your goods all over the world without leaving your office chair?
- ✔ Tap the fastest growing and most affluent market ever?
- ✔ Slash your marketing and advertising costs?
- ✔ Talk to the other side of the world for free?
- ✔ Have access to strategic information only the biggest companies could afford?

Then your business should be on the Internet!

Companies are already cutting costs, improving customer support and reaching hitherto untapped markets via the Internet. They have realised the potential for this exciting new commercial arena and they've grabbed the opportunity with both hands. Now you can join in the fun of what is still a 'ground floor' opportunity.

Starting and Running a Business on The Internet offers realistic and practical advice for any existing business or budding 'Cyberpreneur'. It also:

- ❏ Helps you get started QUICKLY and CHEAPLY.
- ❏ Tells you which sites 'work', which don't and, more importantly, exactly WHY!
- ❏ Details how to PROMOTE your business online.
- ❏ Shows you how to stay ahead of your competitors.
- ❏ Warns you of the major PITFALLS and shows you how to AVOID them.
- ❏ Highlights important issues like CREDIT CARD handling and site SECURITY.

Understand Shares in a Day   Second Edition
Shows how the share market really works. Inexperienced investors will learn: 
● About different types of shares ... ● Why share prices fluctuate... ● How to read the financial pages ... ● How shares are bought and sold ... ● How risk can be spread with investment– and unit trusts ... ● How to build a portfolio of shares ...● The risks and rewards associated with Penny Shares
Once this groundwork has been covered, the book explores more complex ideas which will appeal to both beginners and more experienced investors alike.
£6.95/$11.95

Investing in Options: For the Private Investor
A hardback book which shows you exactly how to 'gear' your money to provide more growth. Step-by-step it teaches how you appraise an options position, looking at the rewards and risks, and then how to execute a deal. There are plenty of examples to show you exactly how its done and how to trade profitably. 
For the experienced options buyer there are examples of option combinations which can be used to create almost any desired outcome.   With options you can make money whichever direction the market is moving.
192 pages   £14.95/$27.50   Hardback

Investing for the Long Term
This book is aimed at those savvy investors who are content to ride out short term fluctuations in the markets in order to realise bigger long term gains. Be it for school fees, a larger house or retirement, if you need money in more than 10 years time, this book is for you. Very comprehensive; covering everything from growth versus income to understanding company accounts, and from downturns, corrections & crashes to looking at the larger economic picture. 
192 pages   £14.95/$27.50   Hardback

Complete Beginner's Guide to the Internet

What exactly is The Internet? Where did it come from and where is it going? And, more importantly, how can everybody take their place in this new community?
The Complete Beginner's Guide to The Internet tells you: ● What types of resources are available for private, educational and business use ● What software and hardware you need to access them ● How to communicate with others, and ● The rules of the Superhighway, known as 'netiquette'. An indispensable guide to the basics of Cyberspace.
£5.95/$9.95

Smart Guide to Microsoft Office 2000

The Smart Guide to Office 2000 is the first in an exciting new popular computing series from Net.Works. It is a basic, easy-to-read introduction to the latest Office suite of applications. Filled with short-cuts and tips, this book gives simple directions to help the reader with: ● Creating formatting, and editing professional-looing documents and charts in Word ● Working with formulas, charts, and spreadsheets using Excel ● Communicating with e-mail using Outlook ● Organising your time and tasks using Outlook ● Using the resources of the World Wide Web with Internet Explorer ● Presenting Powerpoint slide shows ● Creating publications, including newsletters, with Publisher, and ● Working with databases to develop reports in Access.
298 pages   £10.95

Complete Beginner's Guide to Windows 98

You can read The Complete Beginner's Guide to Windows 98 on the train, during your coffee break or while you sit in front of your PC. By the end of each chapter you'll have learned useful skills in Windows 98. By the time you reach the last page you may not get shivers up and down your spine whenever you think of Windows 98, but you'll be using your Windows 98 computer with confidence, working a little bit smarter and having more fun along the way.
£5.95/$9.95

The ***On The Internet*** series provides a detailed listing of the best sites in each category. Site addresses are given and all are reviewed in terms ofcontent, layout and design, as well as the technical aspects such as speed of downloading, and ease of internal navigation. Finallly, the authors let you know which material is free, which you need to pay for an how heavy the advertising is on each site.

Gambling on the Internet
Investment on the Internet
Sex on the Internet
Golf on the Internet

Each Title
£4.95/$9.95

Book Ordering

To order any of these books, please order from our secure website at **www.net-works.co.uk** or complete the form below (or use a plain piece of paper) and send to:

Europe/Asia
TTL, PO Box 200, Harrogate HG1 2YR, England (or fax to 01423-526035, or email: sales@net-works.co.uk).

USA/Canada
Trafalgar Square, PO Box 257, Howe Hill Road, North Pomfret, Vermont 05053 (or fax to 802-457-1913, call toll free 800-423-4525, or email: tsquare@sover.net)

Postage and handling charge:
UK - £1 for first book, and 50p for each additional book
USA - $5 for first book, and $2 for each additional book (all shipments by UPS, please provide street address).
Elsewhere - £3 for first book, and £1.50 for each additional book via surface post (for airmail and courier rates, please fax or email for a price quote)

Book	Qty	Price
	Postage	
	Total	

☐ I enclose a cheque/postal order made payable to 'TTL'
☐ Please debit my VISA/AMEX/MASTERCARD

Number: ☐☐☐☐ ☐☐☐☐ ☐☐☐☐ ☐☐☐☐

Expiry Date: ☐☐☐☐   Signature: _____   Date: _____

Name: _____
Address: _____
_____
_____
Postcode/Zip: _____
Tel/Email: _____

createbk